PRAC

GUIDE TO

FINANCIAL

FREEDOM

&

PEACE

OF MIND

1000

TIMELESS QUOTES & WISDOM KEYS
ON MONEY MATTERS

EDITOR: FRANCIS E.U.

Published by KHARIS PUBLISHING, an imprint of
KHARIS MEDIA LLC.

Copyright © 2024 Francis E. U.

ISBN-13: 978-1-63746-242-3

ISBN-10: 1-63746-242-5

Library of Congress Control Number: 2024931273

All KHARIS PUBLISHING products are available at
special quantity discounts for bulk purchase for sales
promotions, premiums, fund-raising, and educational
needs. For details, contact:

Kharis Media LLC
Tel: 1-630-909-3405
support@kharispublishing.com
www.kharispublishing.com

CONTENTS

WEALTH THROUGH THE AGES:
550BC – 1820AD

1. "Deep doubts, deep wisdom; small doubts, small wisdom." — *Ancient Chinese proverb*

2. "A person can achieve everything by being simple and humble." — *Rig Veda (ancient India)*

3. "So God said to [Solomon], 'Since you have asked for this and not for long life or wealth for yourself, nor have asked for the death of your enemies but for discernment in administering justice, I will do what you have asked. I will give you a wise and discerning heart, so that there will never have been anyone like you, nor will there ever be. Moreover, I will give you what you have not asked for — both wealth and honor — so that in your lifetime you will have no equal among kings.'" — *I Kings 3:11—13*

4. "Everything flows and nothing abides, everything gives way and nothing stays fixed. No man steps in the same river twice, for it is not the same river and he is not the same man" — *Heraclitus* (500 BCE)

5. "Day by day, what you choose, what you think, and what you do is who you become." — *Heraclitus*

6. "Everything flows and nothing abides, everything gives way and nothing stays fixed." — *Heraclitus*

7. "Stretch your arm no further than your sleeve will reach." — *Turkish proverb*

8. A journey of a thousand miles must begin with a single step. — *Lao Tzu (604 — 531 BC)*

9. "Being deeply loved by someone gives you strength while loving someone deeply gives you courage. — *Lao Tzu*

10. "You can't build a reputation on what you're going to do." — **Confucius** *(551—479 BCE)*

11. "What you leave behind is not what is engraved in stone monuments, but what is woven into the lives of others." — *Pericles (495 — 425 BC)*

12. "It is thrifty to prepare today for the wants of tomorrow." —*Aesop*

13. "When rich, think of poverty, but don't think of riches when poor." — *Ancient Chinese proverb*

14. "Lazy hands make for poverty, but diligent hands bring wealth." —*Proverbs 10:4*

15. "Beware the barrenness of a busy life." — *Socrates* (470—399 BC)

16. "He is richest who is content with the least, for contentment is the wealth of nature." — *Socrates*

17. "The only true wisdom is in knowing that you know nothing." — *Socrates*

18. "The greatest wealth is to live content with little." — *Plato* (427—347 BC)

19. "No wealth can ever make a bad man at peace with himself." — *Plato*

20. "Courage is knowing what not to fear." — *Plato*

21. "Necessity is the mother of invention." — *Plato*

22. "Ignorance is the root and stem of all evil." — *Plato*

23. "I count him braver who overcomes his desires than him who conquers his enemies, for the hardest victory is over the self." — *Aristotle (384—322 BC)*

24. "Educating the mind without educating the heart is no education at all." —*Aristotle*

25. "It is the mark of an educated man to be able to entertain a thought without accepting it." —*Aristotle*

26. He best time to plant a tree was twenty years ago; the second best time is now." — *Ancient Chinese proverb*

27. "Laziness erodes a person of his enthusiasm and energy. As a result the person loses all opportunities and becomes dejected and frustrated. The worst thing is that he stops believing in himself." — *Sam Veda* **(Ancient Indian wisdom)**

28. "Ephraim boasts, 'I am very rich. I have become wealthy. With all my wealth, they will not find in me any iniquity or sin.'" — *Hosea 12:8*

29. "But remember the LORD your God, for it is he who gives you the ability to produce wealth, and so confirms his covenant, which he swore to your ancestors, as it is today." *—Deuteronomy 8:18*

30. "Frugality includes all the other virtues." — **Cicero (107 — 44 BC)**

31. "Fortune sides with him who dares." — *Virgil* **(71 — 20 BC)**

32. "Money grows on the tree of persistence." *—Japanese proverb*

33. "It is not the man who has too little, but the man who craves more, that is poor." — *Seneca* **(4 BC — 65 AD)**

34. "It is not the man who has too little, but the man who craves more, that is poor." — *Seneca*

35. "Wealth is the slave of a wise man. The master of a fool" —*Seneca*

36. "Every new beginning comes from some other beginning's end." — *Seneca*

37. "With money, the dog dances." — *Mexican proverb*

38. "The whole life of a man is but a point in time; let us enjoy it. " — *Plutarch* (46 — 119 AD)

39. "Know how to listen and you will profit even from those who speak badly." — *Plutarch*

40. "Wealth consists not in having great possessions, but in having few wants." — *Epictetus* (50 — 138AD)

41. "Make the best use of what's in your power and take the rest as it happens." — *Epictetus*

42. "He is a wise man who does not grieve for the things which he has not but rejoices for those which he has." — *Epictetus*

43. "Be careful to leave your sons well instructed rather than rich, for the hopes of the instructed are better than the wealth of the ignorant." — *Epictetus*

44. "For the love of money is a root of all kinds of evil. Some people, eager for money, have wandered from the faith and pierced themselves with many griefs." — *I Timothy 6:10*

45. "The rich would have to eat money if the poor did not provide food." — *Russian proverb*

46. "The greater danger for most of us lies not in setting our aim too high and falling short; but in setting our aim too low and achieving our mark." — *Michelangelo (1475 — 1564)*

47. "One man to live in pleasure and wealth whilst all other weep and smart for it, that is the part not of a king, but of a jailor." — *Thomas More* (1478 — 1535)

48. "Never stand begging for that which you have the power to earn." — *Miguel de Cervantes* (1547 — 1616)

49. "The gratification of wealth is not found in mere possession or in lavish expenditure, but in its wise application." —*Miguel de Cervantes*

50. "Money is like muck—not good unless it be spread." — *Francis Bacon* (1561 — 1626)

51. "If thou wilt lend this money…lend it rather to thine enemy, who, if he break, thou mayest with better face exact the penalty." — *Antonio, Merchant of Venice, Act I, Scene 3, Shakespeare* (1564 — 1616)

52. "Every good act is charity. A man's true wealth hereafter is the good that he does in this world to his fellows." — *Moliere* **(1622—1673; French playwright and actor)**

53. "Don't think money does everything or you are going to end up doing everything for money." — *Voltaire* (1694 — 1778)

54. "A wise person should have money in their head, but not in their heart." — *Jonathan Swift* (1667—1745)

55. "An investment in knowledge pays the best interest." — *Benjamin Franklin* (1705—1790)

56. "Creditors have better memories than debtors." —*Benjamin Franklin*

57. "Money never made a man happy yet, nor will it. The more a man has, the more he wants. Instead of filling a vacuum, it makes one." — *Benjamin Franklin*

58. "Wealth is not his that has it, but his that enjoys it." — *Benjamin Franklin*

59. "If you would be wealthy…think of saving as well as of getting…Away then with your expensive follies, and you will not have so much cause to complain of hard times, heavy taxes and chargeable families." — *Benjamin Franklin*

60. "Without continual growth and progress, such words as improvement, achievement, and success have no meaning." — *Benjamin Franklin*

61. "Beware of small expenses. A small leak will sink a great ship."— *Benjamin Franklin*

62. "Diligence is the mother of good luck." — *Benjamin Franklin*

63. "The money you have gives you freedom; the money you pursue enslaves you." — *Jean—Jacques Rousseau* (1712 — 1778)

64. "When a fellow says it ain't the money but the principle of the thing, it's the money." — *Artemus Ward* (1727 — 1800)

65. "If we command our wealth, we shall be rich and free. If our wealth commands us, we are poor indeed." —*Edmund Burke* (1729 — 1797

66. "Never spend your money before you have earned it." — *Thomas Jefferson* (1743 — 1826)

67. "I'm a great believer in luck, and I find the harder I work the more I have of it." — *Thomas Jefferson*

68. "Many people take no care of their money till they come nearly to the end of it, and others do just the same with their time." — *Johann Wolfgang von Goethe* (1749 — 1832)

69. "Wealth after all is a relative thing since he that has little and wants less is richer than he that has much and wants more." — *Charles Caleb Colton* (1777 — 1832)

70. "Wealth is like sea—water; the more we drink, the thirstier we become; and the same is true of fame." — *Arthur Schopenhauer* (1788 — 1860)

71. "Wealth is largely the result of habit." — *John Jacob Astor* (1763 — 1848)

72. "Go as far as you can see; when you get there, you'll be able to see further." — *Thomas Carlyle* (1795 — 1891)

73. "If you wish to get rich, save what you get. A fool can earn money, but it takes a wise man to save and dispose of it to his own advantage." — *Brigham Young* **(1801 — 1873)**

74. "Money often costs too much." — *Ralph Waldo Emerson* **(1803 — 1882)**

75. "Do not go where the path may lead, go instead where there is no path and leave a trail." — *Ralph Waldo Emerson*

76. "The first wealth is health." — *Ralph Waldo Emerson*

77. "What you do speaks so loudly that I cannot hear what you say." — *Ralph Waldo Emerson*

78. "Let no feeling of discouragement prey upon you, and in the end you are sure to succeed." — *Abraham Lincoln* **(1809 — 1865)**

79. My old father used to have a saying: If you make a bad bargain, hug it all the tighter. — *Abraham Lincoln*

80. "Give me six hours to chop down a tree and I will spend the first four sharpening the axe." *— Abraham Lincoln*

81. "Money is life's fire: it is a terrible master but an excellent servant." *— P.T. Barnum (1810 — 1891)*

82. "Money is good for nothing unless you know the value of it by experience." *— P.T Barnum*

83. "Never give up, for that is just the time and place that the tide will turn." *— Harriet Beecher Stowe (1811 — 1896)*

84. "Annual income twenty pounds, annual expenditure nineteen six, result happiness. Annual income twenty pounds, annual expenditure twenty pound ought and six, result misery." *— Charles Dickens (1812 — 1870)*

85. "No one is useless in this world who lightens the burdens of another." *— Charles Dickens*

86. "Wealth is the ability to fully experience life." *— Henry David Thoreau (1817 — 1862)*

87. "That man is richest whose pleasures are cheapest." — *Henry David Thoreau*

88. "What you get by achieving your goals is not as important as what you become by achieving your goals." — *Henry David Thoreau*

Wealth Through the Ages: 1821 — 1940: Big Dreams, Big Ideas, Big World

89. "You are no longer a boy, and one of the first duties which a man owes to his friends and to society is to live within his income." *—Thomas Hughes* (1822 — 1896)

90. "I pity that man who wants a coat so cheap that the man or woman who produces the cloth shall starve in the process." — *Benjamin Harrison* (1833 — 1901)

91. Friendship is like money, easier made than kept. — *Samuel Butler* (1835 — 1902)

92. "Twenty years from now you will be more disappointed by the things that you didn't do than by the ones you did do." — *Mark Twain* (1835 — 1910)

93. "Whenever you find yourself on the side of the majority, it is time to pause and reflect." *—Mark Twain*

94. "Buy land. They're not making it anymore." *—Mark Twain*

95. "The best way to save money is to not spend it." *—Mark Twain*

96. "The secret of success lies not in doing your work, but in recognizing the best person to do it." — *Andrew Carnegie* (1839 — 1919)

97. "If you want to get rich, think of saving as earning." — *Andrew Carnegie*

98. "You are what you think. So just think big, act big, work big, give big, forgive big, laugh big, love big, and live big." — *Andrew Carnegie*

99. "Success can be attained in any branch of human labor. There is always room at the top in every pursuit. Concentrate all your thought and energy upon the performance of your duties." — *Andrew Carnegie*

100. "The greatest astonishment of my life was the discovery that the man who does the work is not the man who gets rich." — *Andrew Carnegie*

101. "No person will make a great business who wants to do it all himself or get all the credit." — *Andrew Carnegie*

102. "The average person puts only 25% of his energy and ability into his work. The world takes off its hat to those who put in more than 50% of their capacity and stands on its head for those few and far between souls who devote 100%." — *Andrew Carnegie*

103. "The major fortunes in America have been made in land." — *John D. Rockefeller* **(1839 — 1937)**

104. "If you want to succeed you should strike out on new paths, rather than travel the worn paths of accepted success." — *John D Rockefeller*

105. "Money's a horrid thing to follow, but a charming thing to meet." — *Henry James* **(1843 — 1916)**

106. "Opportunity is missed by most people because it is dressed in overalls and looks like work." — *Thomas A. Edison* (1847 — **1931)**

107. "I have not failed. I've just found 10,000 ways that won't work." — *Thomas A. Edison*

108. "We should remember that good fortune often happens when opportunity meets with preparation." — *Thomas A. Edison*

109. "Our greatest weakness lies in giving up. The most certain way to succeed is always to try just one more time." — *Thomas A. Edison*

110. "It is better to have a permanent income than to be fascinating." — *Oscar Wilde* **(1854 — 1900)**

111. "When I was young I thought money was the most important thing in life, now that I'm old — I know it is!" — *Oscar Wilde*

112. "Success is to be measured not so much by the position that one has reached in life as by the obstacles which he has overcome while trying to succeed." — *Booker T. Washington* **(1856 — 1919)**

113. "If all the economists were laid end to end, they'd never reach a conclusion." — *George Bernard Shaw* **(1856 — 1950)**

114. "Believe you can and you're halfway there."
— *Theodore Roosevelt* **(1858 — 1919)**

115. "No man should receive a dollar unless that dollar has been fairly earned." —*Theodore Roosevelt*

116. "The only man who never makes mistakes is the man who never does anything." — *Theodore Roosevelt*

117. "It is only through labor and painful effort, by grim energy and resolute courage; that we move on to better things." — *Theodore Roosevelt*

118. "It's not the employer who pays the wages. Employers only handle the money. It's the customer who pays the wages."— *Henry Ford* **(1863 — 1947)**

119. "If money is your hope for independence you will never have it. The only real security that a man will have in this world is a reserve of knowledge, experience, and ability." — *Henry Ford*

120. "Whether you think you can or you think you can't, you're right." — *Henry Ford*

121. "If everyone is moving forward together, then success takes care of itself." — *Henry Ford*

122. "I had to make my own living and my own opportunity. But I made it! Don't sit down and wait for the opportunities to come. Get up and make them."— *Madam C.J. Walker* **(1867 — 1919)**

123. "Live as if you were to die tomorrow. Learn as if you were to live forever." — *Mahatma Gandhi* **(1869 — 1948)**

124. "Capital as such is not evil; it is its wrong use that is evil. Capital in some form or other will always be needed." — *Mahatma Gandhi*

125. "Seek not greater wealth, but simpler pleasure; not higher fortune, but deeper felicity." — *Mahatma Gandhi*

126. "For every minute that I spin, there is in me the consciousness that I am adding to the nation's wealth." — *Mohandas Gandhi*

127. "The real voyage of discovery consists in not seeking new landscapes, but in having new eyes." — *Marcel Proust* (1871 — 1922

128. "We make a living by what we get, but we make a life by what we give." — *Winston Churchill* (1874 — 1965)

129. "Success is walking from failure to failure with no loss of enthusiasm." — *Winston Churchill*

130. "You will never reach your destination if you stop and throw stones at every dog that barks." — *Winston Churchill*

131. Too many people spend money they earned…to buy things they don't want…to impress people that they don't like." — *Will Rogers* (1879 — 1935)

132. The quickest way to double your money is to fold it in half and put it in your back pocket. —*Will Rogers*

133. "Don't wait to buy real estate. Buy real estate and wait." — *Will Rogers*

134. "Not everything that can be counted counts, and not everything that counts can be counted." — *Albert Einstein* **(1879 — 1955)**

135. "Compound interest is the eighth wonder of the world. He who understands it, earns it ... he who doesn't ... pays it." — *Albert Einstein*

136. "Happiness is not in the mere possession of money; it lies in the joy of achievement, in the thrill of creative effort." — *Franklin D. Roosevelt* **(1882 — 1945)**

137. "Interest on debts grows without rain." — *Yiddish Proverb*

138. "Formula for success: rise early, work hard, strike oil." — *J. Paul Getty* **(1882 — 1976)**

139. "Buy when everyone else is selling and hold until everyone else is buying. That's not just a catchy slogan. It's the very essence of successful investing." — *J. Paul Getty*

140. "Money is like manure. You have to spread it around, or it smells." —*J. Paul Getty*

141. "Money is like love; it kills slowly and painfully the one who withholds it and enlivens the other who turns it on his fellow man." — *Kahlil Gibran* (1883 — 1931)

142. "He who loses money, loses much; He who loses a friend, loses much more; He who loses faith, loses all." — *Eleanor Roosevelt* (1884 — 1962)

143. "It takes as much energy to wish as it does to plan." — *Eleanor Roosevelt*

144. "Do one thing every day that scares you." — *Eleanor Roosevelt*

145. "The future belongs to those who believe in their dreams." — *Eleanor Roosevelt*

146. "Develop success from failures. Discouragement and failure are two of the surest stepping stones to success." — *Dale Carnegie* (1888 — 1955)

147. "What good is money if it can't buy happiness?" —*Agatha Christie* **(1890 — 1976)**

148. "Empty pockets never held anyone back. Only empty heads and empty hearts can do that." — *Norman Vincent Peale (1898 — 1993)*

149. "Money is only a tool. It will take you wherever you wish, but it will not replace you as the driver." — *Ayn Rand (1905 — 1982)*

150. "The question isn't who is going to let me; it's who is going to stop me." — *Ayn Rand*

151. "If you want to know what a man is really like, take notice of how he acts when he loses money." — *Simone Weil (1909 — 1943)*

152. "Attention is the rarest and purest form of generosity." — *Simone Weil*

153. "The four most expensive words in the English language are, 'This time it's different."' — *Sir John Templeton* (1912— 2008)

154. "It's a kind of spiritual snobbery that makes people think they can be happy without money." —*Albert Camus (1913 — 1960)*

155. "Financial peace of mind is not determined by how much we make but is dependent upon how much we spend." — *Marvin J. Ashton (1915 — 1994)*

156. "Education is the great engine of personal development. It is through education that the daughter of a peasant can become a doctor, that the son of a mineworker can become the head of the mine, that a child of farm workers can become the president of a great nation. It is what we make out of what we have, not what we are given, that separates one person from another." — *Nelson Mandela (1918 — 2013)*

157. "Money won't create success, the freedom to make it will." — *Nelson Mandela*

158. "There is no passion to be found playing small—in settling for a life that is less than the one you are capable of living." — *Nelson Mandela*

159. "I made my money the old—fashioned way. I was very nice to a wealthy relative right before he died." — ***Malcolm Forbes (1919 — 1990)***

160. "This wise man observed that wealth is a tool of freedom. But the pursuit of wealth is the way to slavery." — ***Frank Herbert 1920 — 1986***

161. "Before you speak, listen. Before you write, think. Before you spend, earn. Before you invest, investigate. Before you criticize, wait. Before you pray, forgive. Before you quit, try. Before you retire, save. Before you die, give." — ***William A. Ward*** (1921 — 1994)

162. "A nickel ain't worth a dime anymore." — ***Yogi Berra*** (1925 — 2015)

163. "Get the money honestly if you can." — ***American proverb***

164. "Rich people have small TVs and big libraries, and poor people have small

libraries and big TVs." — *Zig Ziglar* **(1926 — 2012)**

165. It's not the situation, but whether we react (negative) or respond (positive) to the situation that's important. — *Zig Ziglar*

166. People often say that motivation doesn't last. Well, neither does bathing — that's why we recommend it daily. — *Zig Ziglar*

167. "Expect the best. Prepare for the worst. Capitalize on what comes." — *Zig Ziglar*

168. "The function of education is to teach one to think intensively and to think critically. Intelligence plus character — that is the goal of true education." — *Martin Luther King, Jr.* **(1929 — 1968)**

169. "Our lives begin to end the day we become silent about things that matter." — *Martin Luther King, Jr.*

170. "I have decided to stick to love — hatred is too great a burden to bear." — *Martin Luther King, Jr.*

171. "In the end, we will remember not the words of our enemies but the silence of our friends." — *Martin Luther King, Jr.*

172. "We must use time creatively, in the knowledge that the time is always right to do right." — *Martin Luther King, Jr.*

173. Don't tell me what you value, show me your budget, and I'll tell you what you value." — *Joe Biden* (1942 —

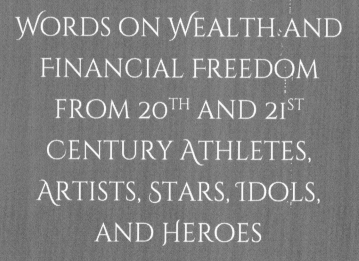

WORDS ON WEALTH AND
FINANCIAL FREEDOM
FROM 20TH AND 21ST
CENTURY ATHLETES,
ARTISTS, STARS, IDOLS,
AND HEROES

174. "The best way to get out of debt is to make a plan and stick to it." — *Alvin Adams, The Money Talks News Podcast*

175. "Sacrifice is a part of life. It's supposed to be. it's not something to regret. It's something to aspire to." — *Mitch Albom*

176. "What you're thinking is what you're becoming." — *Muhammad Ali*

177. "Impossible is just a word thrown around by small men who find it easier to live in the world they've been given than to explore the power they have to change it. Impossible is not a fact. It's an opinion. Impossible is potential. Impossible is temporary. Impossible is nothing." — *Muhammad Ali*

178. "Don't be afraid to ask for help when you need it." — *Tiffany Aliche, The Budgetista*

179. "Pursuing your passion is fulfilling and leads to financial freedom" — *Robert G. Allen*

180. "You may encounter many defeats, but you must not be defeated." — *Maya Angelou*

181. "You can only become truly accomplished at something you love. Don't make money your goal. Instead, pursue the things you love doing, and then do them so well that people can't take their eyes off you." — *Maya Angelou*

182. "When we give cheerfully and accept gratefully, everyone is blessed." — *Maya Angelou*

183. "One important key to success is self—confidence. An important key to self—confidence is preparation." —*Arthur Ashe*

184. "To acquire money requires valor, to keep money requires prudence, and to spend money well is an art." —*Berthold Auerbach, poet*

185. "Do not let the behavior of others destroy your inner peace." —*Jane Austen*

186. "Giving back to those who are less fortunate shows great character and is the right thing to do." — *Cynthia Bailey*

187. "To get rich, you have to be making money while you're asleep." — *David Bailey*

188. "Anything that you learn becomes your wealth, a wealth that cannot be taken away from you; whether you learn it in a building called school or in the school of life. To learn something new is a timeless pleasure and a valuable treasure. And not all things that you learn are taught to you, but many things that you learn you realize you have taught yourself." — *C. Joy Bell*

189. "Try to save something while your salary is small; it's impossible to save after you begin to earn more." — *Jack Benny*

190. "It's amazing how fast later comes when you buy now." — *Milton Berle*

191. "To me, I think leadership is activism. It's giving back to your community, it's investing in oneself, and you know women and children." — *Black Thought*

192. "The best way to look stylish on a budget is to try second—hand, bargain hunting, and vintage." — *Orlando Bloom*

193. "The only point in making money is, you can tell some big shot where to go." — *Humphrey Bogart*

194. "Other things may change us, but we start and end with the family." — *Anthony Brandt*

195. "A successful man is one who can lay a firm foundation with the bricks others have thrown at him." — *David Brinkley*

196. "Remember that the happiest people are not those getting more, but those giving more." — *H. Jackson Brown Jr.*

197. "Success is not the key to happiness. Happiness is the key to success. If you love what you are doing, you will be successful." —*Herman Cain*

198. "Most people work just hard enough not to get fired and get paid just enough money not to quit." — *George Carlin*

199. "I think everybody should get rich and famous and do everything they ever dreamed of so they can see that it's not the answer." — *Jim Carrey*

200. "A leader takes people where they want to go. A great leader takes people where they don't necessarily want to go, but ought to be." — *Rosalynn Carter*

201. "You live but once; you might as well be amusing." — *Coco Chanel*

202. "Giving back has definitely kept me grounded. Stepping outside of yourself to serve a group or community of people who are in need in some facet has a way of doing that. I don't ever want to grow to a place where giving back becomes a foreign concept." — *Karen Civil*

203. "Many folks think they aren't good at earning money, when what they don't know is how to use it." — *Frank A. Clark*

204. "Now I will tell thee an unusual truth about men and sons of men. It is this: That what each of us calls our 'necessary expenses' will always grow to equal our incomes unless we

protest to the contrary." — *George Samual Clason*

205. "Trust yourself. Think for yourself. Act for yourself. Speak for yourself. Be yourself. Imitation is suicide.**" —** *Marva Collins*

206. "The secret of my success is that I make other people money. And, never ever, ever, ever be ashamed about trying to earn as much as possible for yourself, if the person you're working with is also making money. That's life!" — *Simon Cowell*

207. "You don't need to raise money. You need to be smart and be focused." —*Mark Cuban*

208. "Talent without effort is wasted talent. And while the effort is the one thing you can control in your life, applying that effort intelligently is next on the list." — *Mark Cuban*

209. "Nothing in life is to be feared, it is only to be understood. Now is the time to understand more, so that we may fear less." — *Marie Curie*

210. "Financial freedom is a journey, not a destination." — *Aisha Curry, The Aisha Curry Show*

211. "Liking money like I like it, is nothing less than mysticism. Money is glory." — *Salvador Dali*

212. "Family is the most important thing in the world." — *Princess Diana*

213. "There is a gigantic difference between earning a great deal of money and being rich." — *Marlene Dietrich*

214. "Our greatest natural resource is in the minds of our children" — *Walt Disney*

215. "All our dreams can come true if we have the courage to pursue them." — *Walt Disney*

216. "When you are able to shift your inner awareness to how you can serve others, and when you make this the central focus of your life, you will then be in a position to know true miracles in your progress toward prosperity." — *Wayne W. Dyer*

217. "In preparing for battle I have always found that plans are useless, but planning is indispensable." — *Dwight D. Eisenhower*

218. "I don't believe in spending money lavishly, now that I'm making money." —- *Ansel Elgort*

219. "It's easier to feel a little more spiritual with a couple of bucks in your pocket." —- *Craig Ferguson*

220. "Everything is negotiable. Whether or not the negotiation is easy is another thing." — *Carrie Fisher*

221. "Integrity is the essence of everything successful." —*R. Buckminster Fuller*

222. "How wonderful it is that nobody need wait a single moment before starting to improve the world." — *Anne Frank*

223. "Not he who has much is rich, but he who gives much." — *Erich Fromm*

224. "A bank is a place where they lend you an umbrella in fair weather and ask for it back when it begins to rain."— *Robert Frost*

225. "A budget is a tool that helps you track your income and expenses so you can make informed financial decisions." — *The Frugal Black Girl*

226. "You have to set goals that are almost out of reach. If you set a goal that is attainable without much work or thought, you are stuck with something below your true talent and potential." — *Steve Garvey*

227. "Do what you love. When you love your work, you become the best worker in the world." — *Uri Geller*

228. "Life started getting good when I started making money." — *Balthazar Getty*

229. "If plan A fails, remember there are 25 more letters." — *Chris Guillebeau*

230. "In every conceivable manner, the family is a link to our past, a bridge to our future." — *Alex Haley*

231. "In the Middle Ages, the rich spent their money carelessly on extravagant luxuries, whereas peasants lived frugally minding every penny. Today, the tables have turned. The rich take great care managing their assets and investments while the less well go into debt buying cars and televisions they don't really need."— *Yuval Noah Harari*

232. "If you don't know where you're going, any road will get you there." — *George Harrison*

233. "The best way to make more money is to increase your skills and knowledge." — *Chris Hogan, The Chris Hogan Show*

234. "My idea of Christmas, whether old—fashioned or modern, is very simple: loving others. Come to think of it, why do we have to wait for Christmas to do that?" — *Bob Hope*

235. "The first rule of money is to pay yourself first." — *Morgan Housel, author of the Psychology of Money*

236. "Doing well with money has a little to do with how smart you are and a lot to do with how you behave." — *Morgan Housel*

237. "It doesn't matter about money; having it, not having it. Or having clothes, or not having them. You're still left alone with yourself in the end." *— Billy Idol*

238. "Make sure to save for the future and keep making money!" *—Jam Master Jay*

239. "Belief in oneself and knowing who you are … that's the foundation for everything great." *—Jay—Z*

240. "I'm hungry for knowledge. The whole thing is to learn every day, to get brighter and brighter." *—Jay—Z*

241. "It's better to look ahead and prepare than to look back and regret." *— Jackie Joyner—Kersee*

242. "One of the greatest disservices you can do a man is to lend him money that he can't pay back." *—Jesse Jones*

243. "The key to success is failure." *— Michael Jordan*

244. "Talent wins games, but teamwork and intelligence win championships." — *Michael Jordan*

245. "Children are the living messages we send to a time we will not see." *—John F. Kennedy*

246. "The wealth of a soul is measured by how much it can feel... its poverty by how little." *—Sherrilyn Kenyon*

247. "The love of family and the admiration of friends is much more important than wealth and privilege." — *Charles Kuralt*

248. " Yesterday you said tomorrow. Just do it." *—Shia LaBeouf*

249. "Our prime purpose in this life is to help others. And if you can't help them, at least don't hurt them." — *Dalai Lama*

250. "The successful warrior is the average man, with laser—like focus." — *Bruce Lee*

251. "I believe in destiny. But I also believe that you can't just sit back and let destiny happen." — *Spike Lee*

252. "It is time for us to stand and cheer for the doer, the achiever, the one who recognizes the challenge and does something about it."
— Vince Lombardi

253. "The difference between a successful person and others is not a lack of strength, not a lack of knowledge, but rather a lack of will."
— Vince Lombardi

254. "Always remember, your focus determines your reality" *— George Lucas*

255. "Family first, always, no matter what the situation." *— Baker Mayfield*

256. "All I ask is the chance to prove that money can't make me happy." *— Spike Milligan*

257. "Advice changes naturally over time as people change, as society changes, and as the financial world changes. Consistency is important over time but ideas and advice will naturally change given a certain length of time." *— The Money Guys (1/10/2020)*

258. "The richest inheritance any child can have is a stable, loving, disciplined family life." — *Daniel Patrick Moynihan*

259. "Some debts are fun when you are acquiring them, but none are fun when you set about retiring them." *—Ogden Nash, poet*

260. "Success is not the result of making money; earning money is the result of success — and success is in direct proportion to our service." *— Earl Nightingale*

261. "All you need is the plan, the road map, and the courage to press on to your destination." *— Earl Nightingale*

262. "Change will not come if we wait for some other person or some other time. We are the ones we've been waiting for. We are the change that we seek." *— Barack Obama*

263. "Success isn't about how much money you make; it's about the difference you make in people's lives." *— Michelle Obama*

264. "After a certain point, money is meaningless. It ceases to be the goal. The game is what counts." — *Aristotle Onassis*

265. "Within certain limits, it is actually true that the less money you have, the less you worry." — *George Orwell*

266. "We all have dreams. But in order to make dreams come into reality, it takes an awful lot of determination, dedication, self—discipline, and effort." — *Jesse Owens*

267. "The worst enemy to creativity is self—doubt." — *Sylvia Plath*

268. "Never get so busy making a living that you forget to make a life." — *Dolly Parton*

269. "A good plan, violently executed now, is better than a perfect plan next week." — *George Patton*

270. "I've never chased money. It's always been about what I can do to motivate and inspire people." — *Tyler Perry*

271. "It doesn't matter if a million people tell you what you can't do, or if ten million tell you

no. If you get one yes from God that's all you need. — *Tyler Perry*

272. "The Bible says that all things work together for the good of those who love the Lord and are called according to his purpose. I believe that. Because I've seen it all work." — *Tyler Perry*

273. "It takes a week to do a sitcom in Hollywood. I do a show a day in my studio, three or four shows a week." — *Tyler Perry*

274. "Our goals can only be reached through a vehicle of a plan, in which we must fervently believe, and upon which we must vigorously act. There is no other route to success." — *Pablo Picasso*

275. "I'd like to live as a poor man with lots of money." — *Pablo Picasso*

276. "You can't change your financial situation overnight, but you can start making small changes today." — *Jada Pinkett Smith, Red Table Talk*

277. "A dream doesn't become reality through magic; it takes sweat, determination and hard work." — *Colin Powell*

278. "Every day is a bank account, and time is our currency. No one is rich, no one is poor, we've got 24 hours each." — *Christopher Rice*

279. "It's easy to say you don't care about money when you have plenty of it." — *Ransom Riggs*

280. "I always believed that when you follow your heart or your gut, when you really follow the things that feel great to you, you can never lose, because settling is the worst feeling in the world." — *Rihanna*

281. "I bargained with Life for a penny,
and Life would pay no more,
However I begged at evening
When I counted my scanty store;

Life is a just employer.
He gives you what you ask,
But once you have set the wages,
Why, you must bear the task.

I worked for a menial's hire,
Only to learn, dismayed,
That any wage I had asked of Life,
Life would have willingly paid"
— *Jessie B. Rittenhouse*

282. "People say that money is not the key to happiness, but I always figured if you have enough money, you can have a key made."
—*Joan Rivers*

283. "Destiny is as destiny does. If you believe you have no control, then you have no control." —*Wess Roberts*

284. "Money is something we choose to trade our life energy for." — *Vicki Robin*

285. "Financial fitness is not a pipe dream or a state of mind. It's a reality if you are willing to pursue it and embrace it." — **Will Robinson**

286. "Wealth is not about having a lot of money; it's about having a lot of options." — *Chris Rock*

287. "It is our choices, that show what we truly are, far more than our abilities."— *J. K Rowling*

288. "Money may not buy happiness, but I'd rather cry in a Jaguar than on a bus." — *Françoise Sagan*

289. "Volunteering is a great way to look outside your own problems. Giving back to makes you happier by both giving you a sense of purpose and helping to put your problems in perspective." — *Karen Salmansohn*

290. "The only place where success comes before work is in the dictionary." — *Vidal Sassoon*

291. "If saving money is wrong, I don't want to be right!" — *William Shatner*

292. "Las Vegas is the only place I know where money really talks—it says, 'Goodbye'". — *Frank Sinatra*

293. "The value we provide most to others is the same value we appreciate most from others." — *Simon Sinek*

294. "Financial freedom is not about being rich, it's about being in control of your money." — *Michelle Singletary, The Money Girl Podcast*

295. "Investing is the key to building wealth." — *Bola Sokunbi, Her First $100K Podcast*

296. "Follow your intuition." — *Steven Spielberg*

297. "Without leaps of imagination or dreaming, we lose the excitement of possibilities. Dreaming, after all, is a form of planning." — *Gloria Steinem*

298. "You have to go broke three times to learn how to make a living." — *Casey Stengel*

299. "You are never too small to make a difference." — *Greta Thunberg*

300. "The most important aspect of keeping your money is being aware of how much of it you are spending." — *Tiffany 'The Budgetnista' Aliche, author of The One Week Budget*

301. "Acknowledging the good that you already have in your life is the foundation for all abundance." —*Eckhart Tolle*

302. "As long as you're going to be thinking anyway, think big." —*Donald Trump*

303. "A business has to be involving, it has to be fun, and it has to exercise your creative instincts." —*Ted Turner*

304. "The way to achieve your own success is to be willing to help somebody else get it first." —*Iyanla Vanzant*

305. "Making money is art and working is art and good business is the best art." —*Andy Warhol*

306. "You can't save what you don't know you have." —*Kiersten Warren, His & Her Money Podcast*

307. "So many people of wealth understand much more about making and saving money than about using and enjoying it. They fail to live because they are always preparing to live." —*Alan Watts*

308. "There are a great many people accumulating what they think is vast wealth, but it's only money." — *Alan Watts*

309. "Courage is being scared to death but saddling up anyway." — *John Wayne*

310. "I'm not comfortable with comfort. I'm only comfortable when I'm in a place where I'm constantly learning and growing." — *Kanye West*

311. "The first step to financial freedom is to understand your money." — *Jamila White, Money Moves Podcast*

312. "You can be young without money, but you can't be old without it." — *Tennessee Williams*

313. "Be thankful for what you have; you'll end up having more. If you concentrate on what you don't have, you will never, ever have enough." — *Oprah Winfrey*

314. "I feel that luck is preparation meeting opportunity." — *Oprah Winfrey*

315. "Forget about the fast lane. If you really want to fly, harness your power to your passion. Honor your calling. Everybody has one. Trust your heart, and success will come to you." — *Oprah Winfrey*

316. "The reason I've been able to be so financially successful is my focus has never, ever for one minute been money." — *Oprah Winfrey*

317. "What other people label or might try to call failure I have learned is just God's way of pointing you in a new direction" — *Oprah Winfrey*

318. "I am grateful for the blessings of wealth, but it hasn't changed who I am. My feet are still on the ground. I'm just wearing better shoes." — *Oprah Winfrey*

319. "Do the one thing you think you cannot do. Fail at it. Try again. Do better the second time. The only people who never tumble are those who never mount the high wire. This is your moment. Own it."— *Oprah Winfrey*

320. "I am grateful for the blessings of wealth, but it hasn't changed who I am. My feet are still on the ground. I'm just wearing better shoes." —*Oprah Winfrey*

321. "Everyone wants to ride with you in the limo, but what you want is someone who will take the bus with you when the limo breaks down." — *Oprah Winfrey*

322. "If your ship doesn't come in, swim out to meet it!" —*Jonathan Winters*

323. "We all have ability. The difference is how we use it." — *Stevie Wonder*

324. "You cannot find peace by avoiding life." — *Virginia Woolf*

325. "It's not about giving back if you're successful or a celebrity or how much money you have: it's about your responsibility as an adult to help others." — *Trisha Yearwood*

WARREN BUFFET'S RULES OF INVESTMENT AND MAKING MONEY

326. "I will tell you the secret to getting rich on Wall Street. You try to be greedy when others are fearful. And you try to be fearful when others are greedy." — ***Warren Buffett***

327. "The stock market is designed to transfer money from the active to the patient."

328. "The most important of the Warren Buffett quotes:

"Rule No. 1 is never lose money.

Rule No. 2 is never forget Rule No. 1."

329. "Never depend on a single income. Make an investment to create a second source."

330. "Only buy something that you'd be perfectly happy to hold if the market shuts down for ten years."

331. "I never attempt to make money on the stock market. I buy on the assumption that they could close the market the next day and not reopen it for ten years."

332. "If you cannot control your emotions, you cannot control your money."

333. "Forecasts may tell you a great deal about the forecaster; they tell you nothing about the future."

334. "The more you learn, the more you earn."

335. "So smile when you read a headline that says 'Investors lose as market falls. Edit it in your mind to 'Disinvestors lose as market falls—but investors gain. Though writers often forget this truism, there is a buyer for every seller and what hurts one necessarily helps the other."

336. "I will tell you how to become rich. Close the doors. Be fearful when others are greedy. Be greedy when others are fearful.

337. "In the short term, the market is a popularity contest. In the long term, the market is a weighing machine. "

338. "We always live in an uncertain world. What is certain is that the United States will go forward over time."

339. "I don't look to jump over seven—foot bars; I look around for one—foot bars that I can step over.

340. "If you aren't thinking about owning a stock for 10 years, don't even think about owning it for 10 minutes."

341. "Short—term price fluctuation is not the real risk. It is an opportunity."

342. "All there is to investing is picking good stocks at good times and staying with them as long as they remain good companies."

343. "The most important quality for an investor is temperament, not intellect. You need a temperament that neither derives great pleasure from being with the crowd or against the crowd."

344. "It's far better to buy a wonderful company at a fair price, than a fair company at a wonderful price."

345. "Our favorite holding period is forever."

346. "For the investor, a too—high purchase price for the stock of an excellent company can undo the effects of a subsequent decade of favorable business developments."

347. "Wall Street is the only place that people ride to in a Rolls Royce to get advice from those who take the subway."

348. "Of the billionaires I have known, money just brings out the basic traits in them. If they were jerks before they had money, they are simply jerks with a billion dollars."

349. "Wide diversification is only required when investors do not understand what they are doing.

350. "Calling someone who trades actively in the market an investor is like calling someone who repeatedly engages in one—night stands a romantic."

351. "Don't pass up something that's attractive today because you think you will find something better tomorrow."

352. "Widespread fear is your friend as an investor because it serves up bargain purchases."

353. "It's been an ideal period for investors: A climate of fear is their best friend. Those who invest only when commentators are upbeat end up paying a heavy price for meaningless reassurance."

354. "For 240 years, it's been a terrible mistake to bet against America, and now is no time to start."

355. "Lose money for the firm, and I will be understanding. Lose a shred of reputation for the firm, and I will be ruthless."

"If you get to my age in life and nobody thinks well of you, I don't care how big your bank account is, your life is a disaster."

356. "Buy a stock the way you would buy a house. Understand and like it such that you'd be content to own it in the absence of any market."

357. "Investing is a way of putting money to work for you. When you invest, you are buying a piece of a company or a piece of real estate. The goal is to make money over time."

358. "It's far better to buy a wonderful company at a fair price, than a fair company at a wonderful price."

ROBERT KIYOSAKI
FINANCIAL FREEDOM
QUOTES

359. "It's not how much money you make, but how much money you keep, how hard it works for you, and how many generations you keep it for." — **Robert Kiyasoki**

360. "Making money is a common sense. It's not rocket science. But unfortunately, when it comes to money, common sense is uncommon."

361. "Don't let the fear of losing be greater than the excitement of winning."

362. "If you want to be financially free, you need to become a different person than you are today and let go of whatever has held you back in the past."

363. "If you want to be rich, you have to start thinking like a rich person."

364. "The rich invest in assets. The poor invest in liabilities."

365. "Financial freedom is mental, emotional, and education process."

366. "More important than how we achieve financial freedom is the why. Find your reasons why you want to be free and wealthy."

367. "To obtain financial freedom, one must be either a business owner, an investor or both, generating passive income, particularly on a monthly basis."

368. "Financial freedom is available to those who learn about it and work for it."

369. "Financial freedom is freedom from fear."

370. "Financial independence is about having more choices."

371. "The philosophy of the rich and the poor is this: the rich invest their money and spend what is left. The poor spend their money and invest what is left."

372. "The key to financial freedom and great wealth is a person's ability or skill to convert earned income into passive income and/or portfolio income."

373. "The biggest risk a person can take is to do nothing."

374. "The main reason people struggle financially is because they have spent years in school but learned nothing about money. The result is that people learn to work for money...but never learn to have money work for them."

375. "Success takes an investment in time, dedication, and sacrifice. This is true education. It is a process."

376. "Friends and family will tell you why your ideas won't work. Most are left—brained employees and specialists and NOT entrepreneurs."

377. "A lot of people do not invest in business. They invest in busy—ness (They purchase a job.)."

378. "Remember, your mind is your greatest asset, so be careful what you put into it."

379. "Never say you cannot afford something. That is a poor man's attitude. Ask HOW to afford it."

380. "If you want to change your life, begin by changing your words. Start speaking the words of your dreams, of who you want to become, not the words of fear or failure."

381. "We all have defining moments. It is in these moments that we find our true characters. We become heroes or cowards; truth tellers or liars; we go forward or we go backward."

382. "A job is a short term solution to a long term problem."

383. "Before you invest in something, invest the time to understand it."

384. "You don't achieve success by 'taking it easy' or 'working on it later.' You achieve it thru persistence and hard work."

385. "In school we learn that mistakes are bad, and we are punished for making them. Yet, if you look at the way humans are designed to learn, we learn by making mistakes. We learn to walk by falling down. If we never fell down, we would never walk."

386. "Great opportunities are not seen with your eyes. They are seen with your mind."

387. "The rich buy assets. The poor only have expenses. The middle class buys liabilities they think are assets. The poor and the middle class work for money. The rich have money work for them."

388. "If you want a solid future, you need to create it. You can take charge of your future only when you take control of your income source. You need your own business."

DAVE RAMSEY FINANCIAL
FREEDOM QUOTES

389. "You must gain control over your money or the lack of it will forever control you." —
Dave Ramsey

390. "Financial peace isn't the acquisition of stuff. It's learning to live on less than you make, so you can give money back and have money to invest. You can't win until you do this." "Money moves from those who do not manage it to those who do."

391. "You must gain control over your money or the lack of it will forever control you."

392. "A budget is telling your money where to go instead of wondering where it went."

393. "Debt is normal. Be weird."

394. "Live below your means and invest the difference."

395. "The best way to get out of debt is to create a budget and stick to it."

396. "If you don't have a budget, you're not in control of your money. Your money is in control of you."

397. "You must gain control over your money or the lack of it will forever control you."

398. "I believe that through knowledge and discipline, financial peace is possible for all of us."

399. "If you will make the sacrifices now that most people aren't willing to make, later on you will be able to live as those folks will never be able to live."

400. "Act your wage."

401. "Work is doing it. Discipline is doing it every day. Diligence is doing it well every day."

402. "You have the clean canvas of a whole week before you. Paint well."

403. "When getting help with money, whether it is insurance, real estate or investments you should always look for a person with the heart of a teacher, not the heart of a salesman."

404. "Debt gives you the ability to look like you're winning when you're not."

405. "Live like no one else, so later you can live like no one else."

406. "The paid—off home mortgage has taken the place of the BMW as the status symbol of choice."

407. "There's not a party, a congressman, a senator, etc. elected that will fix your life. YOU have to fix YOUR life."

408. "I think the lie we've told people in the marketplace is that a degree gets you a job. A degree doesn't get you a job. What gets you a job is the ability to carry yourself into that room and shake a hand and look someone in the eye and have people skills. These are the things that cause people to become successful."

409. "Work—get paid; don't work—don't get paid. Everybody is on commission."

410. "Disability insurance protects you and your family if you are unable to work by providing income which will help pay your bills and take care of your family. It's just as important as life insurance."

411. "What to do isn't the problem; doing it is. Most of us know what to do, but we just don't do it. If I can control the guy in the mirror, I can be skinny and rich."

412. "The average millionaire can't tell you who got thrown off the island last night."

413. "The German root word for 'debt' is the same as for 'guilt.'"

414. "The lottery is a tax on poor people and on people who can't do math. Rich people and smart people would be in the line if the lottery were a real wealth—building tool, but the truth is that the lottery is a rip—off instituted by our government. This is not a moral position; it is a mathematical, statistical fact. Studies show that the zip codes that spend four times what anyone else does on lottery tickets are those in lower—income parts of town. The lottery, or gambling of any kind, offers false hope, not a ticket out."

JIM ROHN FINANCIAL
FREEDOM QUOTES

415. "Time is more valuable than money. You can get more money, but you cannot get more time." — *Jim Rohn*

416. "Formal education will make you a living; self—education will make you a fortune."

417. "The rich invest their money and spend what is left; the poor spend their money and invest what is left."

418. "Let others lead small lives, but not you. Let others argue over small things, but not you. Let others cry over small hurts, but not you. Let others leave their future in someone else's hands, but not you."

419. "All good men and women must take responsibility to create legacies that will take the next generation to a level we could only imagine."

420. "To become financially independent, you must turn part of your income into capital; turn capital into enterprise; turn enterprise into profit; turn a profit into an investment and turn the investment into financial independence."

421. "If you are not financially independent by the time you are forty or fifty, it doesn't mean that you are living in the wrong country or at the wrong time. It simply means that you have the wrong plan."

422. "When the why gets stronger, the how gets easier."

423. "We suffer one of two things. Either the pain of discipline or the pain of regret. You've got to choose discipline, versus regret, because discipline weighs ounces and regret weighs tons."

424. "The major value in life is not what you get. The major value in life is what you become."

425. "Don't wish it was easier, wish you were better. Don't wish for less problems, wish for more skills. Don't wish for less challenges, wish for more wisdom. The major value in life is not what you get. The major value in life is what you become. Success is not to be pursued; it is to be attracted by the person you become."

426. "If you don't design your own life plan, chances are you'll fall into someone else's plan. And guess what they have planned for you? Not much."

427. "Don't let your learning lead to knowledge. Let your learning lead to action."

428. "The problem with waiting until tomorrow is that when it finally arrives, it is called today."

429. "Good service leads to multiple sales. If you take good care of your customers, they will open doors you could never open by yourself."

430. "To make progress you must actually get started. The key is to take a step today."

431. "Take care of your body. It's the only place you have to live."

432. "Work harder on yourself than you do on your job. If you work hard on your job, you can make a living. If you work hard on yourself, you can make a fortune... Income seldom exceeds personal development."

433. "Excuses are the nails used to build a house of failure."

434. "If you want to have more, you have to become more."

435. "For things to change, you have to change."

436. "For things to get better, you have to become better."

437. "If you improve, everything will improve for you."

438. "If you grow, your money will grow; your relationships, your health, your business and every external effect will mirror that growth in equal correlation."

439. "Discipline has within it the potential for creating future miracles."

440. "You have two choices: You can make a living, or you can design a life."

441. "Profits are better than wages. Wages make you a living; profits make you a fortune."

442. "Work hard at your job and you can make a living. Work hard on yourself and you can make a fortune."

443. "The most important question to ask on the job is not 'What am I getting?' The most important question to ask on the job is 'What am I becoming?'"

444. "The rich invest their money and spend what is left; the poor spend their money and invest what is left."

445. "To succeed in sales, simply talk to lots of people every day. And here's what's exciting: There are lots of people!"

446. "Start from wherever you are and with whatever you've got."

447. "The future does not get better by hope, it gets better by plan. And to plan for the future we need goals."

448. "What is easy to do is also easy not to do."

449. "Learn how to turn frustration into fascination. You will learn more being fascinated by life than you will by being frustrated by it."

450. "Days are expensive. When you spend a day you have one less day to spend. So make sure you spend each one wisely."

WEALTH AND FINANCIAL FREEDOM QUOTES FROM THE WELL—KNOWN AND UNKNOWN

451. "Someone's sitting in the shade today because someone planted a tree a long time ago."

452. "If you aren't willing to own a stock for 10 years, don't even think about owning it for 10 minutes."

453. "Our favorite holding period is forever."

454. "The key to investing is not assessing how much an industry is going to affect society, or how much it will grow, but rather determining the competitive advantage of any given company and, above all, the durability of that advantage."

455. "The most important thing to do if you find yourself in a hole is to stop digging."

456. "Price is what you pay, value is what you get."

457. "The three most important words in investing are 'margin of safety.'"

458. "It's far better to buy a wonderful company at a fair price, than a fair company at a wonderful price."

459. "Beware the investment activity that produces applause; the great moves are usually greeted by yawns."

460. "The business schools reward difficult complex behavior more than simple behavior, but simple behavior is more effective."

461. "Risk comes from not knowing what you are doing."

462. "It is a terrible mistake for investors with long—term horizons — among them pension funds, college endowments, and savings—minded individuals — to measure their investment 'risk' by their portfolio's ratio of bonds to stocks."

463. "Remember that the stock market is a manic depressive."

464. "Do not take yearly results too seriously. Instead, focus on four— or five—year averages."

465. "Never invest in a business you cannot understand."

466. "The most important investment you can make is in yourself."

467. "Never depend on a single income. Make an investment to create a second source."

468. "No matter how great the talent or effort, some things just take time. You can't produce a baby in one month by getting nine women pregnant."

469. "Today people who hold cash equivalents feel comfortable. They shouldn't. They have opted for a terrible long—term asset, one that pays virtually nothing and is certain to depreciate in value."

470. "We never want to count on the kindness of strangers in order to meet tomorrow's obligations. When forced to choose, I will not trade even a night's sleep for the chance of extra profits."

471. "Don't pass up something that's attractive today because you think you will find something better tomorrow."

472. "When trillions of dollars are managed by Wall Streeters charging high fees, it will usually be the managers who reap outsized profits, not the clients."

473. "The best chance to deploy capital is when things are going down."

474. "Opportunities come infrequently. When it rains gold, put out the bucket, not the thimble."

475. "Wall Street is the only place that people ride to in a Rolls Royce to get advice from those who take the subway."

476. "To achieve what one percent of the world's population has (Financial Freedom), you must be willing to do what only one percent dares to do. Hard work and perseverance of highest order."

477. "The struggle for financial freedom is very unfair. Just look at the rewards."

478. "Financial Freedom is less about financials and more about freedom."

479. "You can make excuses and earn sympathy, or you can make money and earn admiration. The choice is always yours…"

480. "You do pay a price for your financial freedom, but it is far lesser than what you pay for a lifetime of slavery."

481. "Financial freedom is the power to produce wealth and not necessarily having wealth." — *Stephen Covey*

482. "The key is not to prioritize what's on your schedule, but to schedule your priorities." — *Stephen Covey*

483. "Your economic security does not lie in your job; it lies in your own power to produce—to think, to learn, to create, to adapt. That's true financial independence. It's not having wealth it's having the power to produce wealth." —*Stephen Covey*

484. "Real wealth is not about money. Real wealth is: not having to go to meetings, not having to spend time with jerks, not being locked into status games, not feeling like you have to say 'yes,' not worrying about others

claiming your time and energy. Real wealth is about freedom." —*James Clear*

485. "Like Warren, I had a considerable passion to get rich, not because I wanted Ferraris — I wanted the independence. I desperately wanted it." — *Charlie Munger*

486. "The habit of saving is itself an education; it fosters every virtue, teaches self-–denial, cultivates the sense of order, trains to forethought, and so broadens the mind." — *T.T. Munger*

487. If you took our top fifteen decisions out, we'd have a pretty average record. It wasn't hyperactivity, but a hell of a lot of patience. You stuck to your principles and when opportunities came along, you pounced on them with vigor. — *Charlie Munger*

488. "Invest in a business any fool can run, because someday a fool will." — *Charlie Munger*

489. "The 'know—nothing' investor should practice diversification, but it is crazy if you are an expert." — *Charlie Munger*

490. "Waiting helps you as an investor and a lot of people just can't stand to wait. If Tony didn't get the deferred—gratification gene, you've got to work very hard to overcome that." — *Charlie Munger*

491. "Working because you want to and not because you have to is financial freedom." — *Tony Robbins*

492. "You either master money, or, on some level, money masters you." — *Tony Robbins*

493. "The secret to wealth is simple: Find a way to do more for others than anyone else does. Become more valuable. Do more. Give more. Be more. Serve more." — *Tony Robbins*

494. "Rich people believe 'I create my life.' Poor people believe 'Life happens to me.'" — *T. Harv Eker*

"My definition of financial freedom is simple: it is the ability to live the lifestyle you desire without having to work or rely on anyone else for money." — *T. Harv Eker*

495. "It's simple arithmetic: "Your income can grow only to the extent you do". — *T. Harv Eker*

496. "At least eighty percent of millionaires are self—made. That is, they started with nothing but ambition and energy, the same way most of us start." — *Brian Tracy*

497. "Financial security and independence are like a three—legged stool resting on savings, insurance, and investments." — *Brian Tracy*

498. "All successful people men and women are big dreamers. They imagine what their future could be, ideal in every respect, and then they work every day toward their distant vision, that goal or purpose." — *Brian Tracy*

499. "The goal isn't more money. The goal is living life on your terms." — *Chris Brogan*

500. "If you're saving, you're succeeding." — *Steve Burkholder*

501. "Financial planning and discipline is key to one's financial freedom." — *Kishorkumar Balpalli*

502. "Millions wish for financial freedom, but only those that make it a priority have millions." — *Oscar Auliq—Ice*

503. "The speed of your success is limited only by your dedication and what you're willing to sacrifice." — *Nathan W. Morris*

504. "Every time you borrow money, you're robbing your future self." — *Nathan W. Morris*

505. "The secret to creating lasting financial change is to decide to pay yourself first and then make it automatic." — *David Bach*

506. "Whatever your income, always live below your means." — *Thomas J. Stanley*

507. "Before you can become a millionaire, you must learn to think like one. You must learn how to motivate yourself to counter fear with courage." — *Thomas J. Stanley*

508. "The person who doesn't know where his next dollar is coming from usually doesn't know where his last dollar went."

509. "Money does not buy you happiness, but lack of money certainly buys you misery." — *Daniel Kahneman*

511. "It's good to have money and the things that money can buy, but it's good, too, to check up once in a while and make sure that you haven't lost the things that money can't buy." — *George Lorimer*

512. "I don't pay good wages because I have a lot of money; I have a lot of money because I pay good wages." — *Robert Bosch*

513. "Money is multiplied in practical value depending on the number of W's you control in your life: what you do, when you do it, where you do it and with whom you do it. I call this the 'freedom multiplier.'" — *Tim Ferriss*

514. "The real measure of your wealth is how much you'd be worth if you lost all your money."

515. "Earn with your mind, not your time." — *Naval Ravikant*

516. "A simple fact that is hard to learn is that the time to save money is when you have some."
— Joe Moore

517. "Know what you own and know why you own it." *— Peter Lynch*

518. "Money isn't everything…but it ranks right up there with oxygen." *— Rita Davenport*

519. "Don't tell me where your priorities are. Show me where you spend your money and I'll tell you what they are." *— James W. Frick*

520. "Every time you borrow money, you're robbing your future self." *— Nathan W. Morris*

521. "Investing should be more like watching paint dry or watching grass grow. If you want excitement, take $800 and go to Las Vegas." *— Paul Samuelson*

522. "There is only one boss. The customer. And he can fire everybody in the company from the chairman on down, simply by spending his money somewhere else."— *Sam Walton*

523. "If you don't value your time, neither will others. Stop giving away your time and talents. Value what you know & start charging for it." — *Kim Garst*

524. "If you want to get rich, remember that the way to do it is via equity, not salary." — *Sam Altman*

525. "The individual investor should act consistently as an investor and not as a speculator." — *Ben Graham*

526. "If you are shopping for common stocks, choose them the way you would buy groceries, not the way you would buy perfume." — *Benjamin Graham*

527. "It's how you deal with failure that determines how you achieve success." — *David Feherty*

528. "What we really want to do is what we are really meant to do. When we do what we are meant to do, money comes to us, doors

open for us, we feel useful, and the work we do feels like play to us." —*Julia Cameron*

529. It's good to have money and the things that money can buy, but it's good, too, to check up once in a while and make sure that you haven't lost the things that money can't buy. — *George Lorimer*

530. "How many millionaires do you know who have become wealthy by investing in savings accounts? I rest my case." — *Robert G. Allen*

531. "The real measure of your wealth is how much you'd be worth if you lost all your money."

532. "Investing should be more like watching paint dry or watching grass grow. If you want excitement, take $800 and go to Las Vegas." — *Paul Samuelson*

533. "Every time you borrow money, you're robbing your future self. "— *Nathan W. Morris*

534. "The stock market is filled with individuals who know the price of everything, but the value of nothing." — *Phillip Fisher*

535. "If you don't value your time, neither will others. Stop giving away your time and talents. Value what you know & start charging for it." — *Kim Garst*

536. "Here's to the crazy ones. The misfits. The rebels. The troublemakers. The round pegs in the square holes. The ones who see things differently. They're not fond of rules. And they have no respect for the status quo. You can quote them, disagree with them, glorify or vilify them. About the only thing you can't do is ignore them. Because they change things. They push the human race forward. And while some may see them as the crazy ones, we see genius. Because the people who are crazy enough to think they can change the world, are the ones who do." –– *Steve Jobs*

537. "Innovation distinguishes between a leader and a follower." — *Steve Jobs*

538. "The only way to do great work is to love what you do." — *Steve Jobs*

539. "Remembering you are going to die is the best way I know to avoid the trap of thinking you have something to lose. You are already naked. There is no reason not to follow your heart." — *Steve Jobs*

540. "Be a yardstick of quality. Some people aren't used to an environment where excellence is expected." — *Steve Jobs*

541. "You can't connect the dots looking forward; you can only connect them looking backwards. So you have to trust that the dots will somehow connect in your future. You have to trust in something — your gut, destiny, life, karma, whatever. This approach has never let me down, and it has made all the difference in my life." — *Steve Jobs*

542. Here's to the crazy ones. The misfits. The rebels. The troublemakers. The round pegs in the square holes. The ones who see things differently. They're not fond of rules. And they have no respect for the status quo. You can quote them, disagree with them, glorify or vilify them. About the only thing you can't do is ignore them. Because they change things. They push the human race forward. And while some may see them as the crazy ones, we see genius. Because the people who are crazy enough to think they can change the world, are the ones who do. — *Steve Jobs*

543. You can't connect the dots looking forward; you can only connect them looking backwards. So you have to trust that the dots will somehow connect in your future. You have to trust in something — your gut, destiny, life, karma, whatever. This approach has never let me down, and it has made all the difference in my life. — *Steve Jobs*

544. "If you live for having it all, what you have is never enough." — *Vicki Robin*

545. "Before you speak, listen. Before you write, think. Before you spend, earn. Before you invest, investigate. Before you criticize, wait. Before you pray, forgive. Before you quit, try. Before you retire, save. Before you die, give." — *William A. Ward*

546. Let him who would enjoy a good future waste none of his present. — *Roger Babson*

547. A real entrepreneur is somebody who has no safety net underneath them. — *Henry Kravis*

548. I'm only rich because I know when I'm wrong…I basically have survived by recognizing my mistakes. — *George Soros*

549. Persist — don't take no for an answer. If you're happy to sit at your desk and not take any risk, you'll be sitting at your desk for the next 20 years. — *David Rubenstein*

550. When buying shares, ask yourself, would you buy the whole company? — *Rene Rivkin*

551. If you have trouble imagining a 20% loss in the stock market, you shouldn't be in stocks. — *John Bogle*

552. "Don't look for the needle in the haystack. Just buy the haystack." — *Jack Bogle*

553. "The best thing money can buy is financial freedom." —*Rob Berger*

554. "Wealth does not make people happy, but positive increases in wealth may."

— *Nassim Nicholas Taleb*

555. "99% of all problems can be solved by money — and for the other 1% there's alcohol." — *Quentin R. Bufogle*

556. "Spend your money on the things money can buy. Spend your time on the things money can't buy." — *Haruki Murakami*

557. "The fools in life want things fast and easy — money, success, attention." —*Robert Greene*

558. "Remember that the only purpose of money is to get you what you want, so think hard about what you value and put it above money." — *Ray Dalio*

559. "A sign of wealth: No longer needing an alarm clock to wake up." — *Greg Isenberg*

560. "Real wealth is not about money. Real wealth is: not having to go to meetings, not having to spend time with jerks, not being locked into status games, not feeling like you have to say "yes", not worrying about others claiming your time and energy. Real wealth is about freedom." —*James Clear*

561. "How many millionaires do you know who have become wealthy by investing in savings accounts? I rest my case. — *Robert G. Allen*

562. "The real measure of your wealth is how much you'd be worth if you lost all your money."

563. "Be master of your petty annoyances and conserve your energies for the big, worthwhile things. It isn't the mountain ahead that wears you out — it's the grain of sand in your shoe." —*Robert Service*

564. "Create a set of great personal values and surround yourself with the right people that can form your support system. Have an optimistic spirit and develop a strong purpose that you completely believe in and everything you can imagine is possible, for you." —*Andrew Horton*

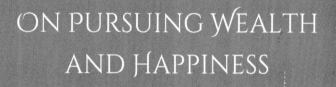

ON PURSUING WEALTH
AND HAPPINESS

565. "Money is neither my god nor my devil. It is a form of energy that tends to make us more of who we already are, whether it's greedy or loving." —*Dan Millman*

566. " Lost wealth may be replaced by industry, lost knowledge by study, lost health by medicine, but lost time is gone forever."

567. "There need to be reasons to get up in the morning." —*Elon Musk*

568. "If you can get up in the morning and think the future is going to be better, it is a bright day. Otherwise, it's not." — *Elon Musk*

569. "I don't think you can cheat on a person you love and if you do, you never loved them fully; otherwise there wouldn't be any voids to fill."

570. "Those who think money can't buy happiness just don't know where to shop . . . People would be happier, and in the long run and wealthier, if they bought basic functional appliances, automobiles, and wristwatches, and invested the money they saved for future consumption; yet

Americans in particular, spend almost everything they have—and sometimes more—on goods for present consumption, often paying a large premium for designer names and superfluous features." — *Jonathan* **Haidt**

571. "I can't give you a sure—fire formula for success, but I can give you a formula for failure: try to please everybody all the time."

572. "[He would question]:What can I learn from this challenge? What is it teaching me? 'Then he would stay positive and trust that the lessons would make him stronger, wiser, and better."

573. "True success, true happiness, lies in freedom and fulfillment." — *Dada Vaswani*

574. "Innocent pleasures are got by virtue and well—earned wealth." — *Dayananda Saraswati*

575. "Create a set of great personal values and surround yourself with the right people that can form your support system. Have an optimistic spirit and develop a strong

purpose that you completely believe in and everything you can imagine is possible, for you." —*Andrew Horton*

576. "We have to innovate for a specific reason, and that reason comes from the market. Otherwise, we'll end up making museum pieces." — *Phil Knight*

577. " Happiness is a state of inner fulfillment." — *Matthieu Richad*

578. "Sacrifice a few years of comfort for decades of freedom." — *Zach Pogorob*

579. "If you were to ask me to choose between democratic values and wealth, power, prosperity and fame, I will very easily and without any doubt choose democratic values." — *Narendra Modi*

580. "You do not find the happy life, you make it." — *Camilla Eyring Kimball*

581. "Freedom is never given, it is won." — *Philip Randolph*

582. "*Perhaps* the single most important ingredient in all life for achieving happiness and fulfillment: Purpose." — *Harvey Volson*

583. "If you want to make your dreams come true, the first thing you have to do is wake up." —*J. M. Power*

584. "View money and things not as something you create to fill a lack, but as tools to help you more fully express yourself and realize your potential." —*Sanaya Roman and Duane Packer*

585. "Both abundance and lack exist simultaneously in our lives, as parallel realities. It is always our conscious choice which secret garden we will tend… when we choose to be grateful for the abundance that's present — love, health, family, friends, work, the joys of nature and personal pursuits that bring us pleasure — the wasteland of lack falls away and we experience heaven on Earth." —*Sarah Ban Breathnach*

586. "Wealth and power don't go together. Power cannot be brokered. To me, power is responsibility." — *Nita Amban*

587. "If you don't educate yourself, you'll never get out of the starting block because you'll spend all your money making foolish decisions." — *Daymond John*

588. "The only thing more expensive than education is ignorance." — *Daymond John*

589. "In investing, what is comfortable is rarely what is profitable." — *Robert Arnot*

590. "Money can't buy happiness but it sure is a stress reliever." — *Besa Kosova*

591. "Destiny is as destiny does. If you think you have no control, then you have no control." — *Wess Roberts*

592. "You are not too old and it is not too late."

593. "Only when the last tree has died and the last river has been poisoned and the last fish has been caught will we realize we cannot eat money." — *Indian proverb*

594. "Rise up, wise up, say it loud: Soul, I will not lie to you. I'm all alone. I'm still missing you…" — *Tegan Quin*

595. "Money can't buy happiness but it will certainly get you a better class of memories." — *Ronald Reagan*

596. "Make glorious, amazing mistakes." — *Neil Gaiman*

597. "My guiding principle is that prosperity can be shared. We can create wealth together. The global economy is not a zero—sum game." — *Julia Gillard*

598. "We are stronger when we listen, and smarter when we share." — *Rania Al—Abdullah*

599. "It is only possible to live happily ever after on a day—to—day basis." — *Margaret Wander Bonano*

600. "Living our life deeply and with happiness, having time to care for our loved ones — this is another kind of success, another kind of power, and it is much more important."

601. "If the risk is fully aligned with your purpose and mission, then it's worth considering." — *Peter Diamandis*

602. "Above all, don't fear difficult moments. The best comes from them." — *Rita Levi—Montalcini*

603. "Your path is at your feet whether you realize it or not." — *Agnes Martin*

604. "The clouds may drop down titles and estates, and wealth may seek us, but wisdom must be sought." — *Edward* **Young**

605. "The difference between successful people and very successful people is that very successful people say 'no' to almost everything."

606. "It is impossible for you to go on as you were before, so you must go on as you never have." — *Cheryl Strayed*

607. "Right actions for the future are the best apologies for wrong ones in the past." — *Tryon Edwards*

608. "Nobody grows old merely by living a number of years. We grow old y deserting our ideals. Years may wrinkle the skin, but to give up enthusiasm wrinkles the soul." — *Frank Crane*

609. "Excuse em while I save, invest, and build wealth." — *Stephanie Lahart*

610. "I believe the second half of one's life is meant to be better than the first half. The first half is finding out how you do it. And the second half is enjoying it." — *Frances Lear*

611. "The really important kind of freedom involves attention, and awareness, and discipline, and effort, on being able truly to care about other people and to sacrifice for them, over and over, in myriad petty little unsexy ways, every day." — *David Foster Wallace*

612. "Gratitude makes sense of our past, brings peace for today, and creates a vision for tomorrow." — *Melody Beattie*

613. "Be charitable before wealth makes you covetous." — *Thomas Browne*

614. "Purposeful giving is not apt to deplete one's resources; it belongs to that natural order of giving that seems to renew itself even in the act of depletion. The more one gives, the more one has to give." — *Anne Morrow Lindbergh*

615. "The time to make up your mind about people is never." — *Philip Barry*

616. "If we don't change, we don't grow. If we don't grow, we are not really living." — *Gail Sheehy*

617. "Unless you are completely retired, earning money is the best form of wealth preservation." — *Felix Dennis*

618. "Success is never accidental."

619. "My grandfather was a Methodist preacher, and my father was an unsuccessful businessman. We didn't have status or wealth." — *Alexandra Stoddard*

620. "Some members of the ruling class are making a concerted effort to expand the wealth gap." — *Tom Steyer*

621. "Capitalism and market forces are very powerful in producing wealth and innovation. But we need to ensure that these forces act in common interest." — *Thomas Piketty*

622. "Find someone to be successful for. Raise their hopes. Think of their needs."

623. "The more money he has the more troubles he will have." — *Charles H. Spurgeon*

624. "Discernment does not mean knowing the difference between right and wrong. Discernment means knowing the difference between what is right and what is almost right." — *Charles H. Spurgeon*

625. "Everyday is a bank account, and time is our currency. No one is rich, no one is poor, we've got 24 hours each." — *Christopher Rice*

ON ATTAINING
WEALTH

626. "It is not in everyone's power to secure wealth, office, or honors; but everyone may be good, generous, and wise." *—Luc De Clapiers*

627. "The tragedy of life doesn't lie in not reaching your goal. The tragedy lies in having no goal to reach." *—Benjamin E. Mayes*

628. "When we feel stuck, going nowhere — even starting to slip backward — we may actually be backing up to get a running start." *—Dan Millman*

629. "Be ready when opportunity comes…. Luck is when preparation and opportunity meet." *—Roy D. Chapin Jr.*

630. "Adversity causes some men to break, and others to break records."

631. "People inspire you or they drown you. Pick them wisely." *— Hans F. Hasen*

632. "What is opportunity, and when does it knock? It never knocks. You can wait a whole lifetime, listening, hoping, and you will hear no knocking. None at all. You are opportunity, and you must knock on the door leading to your destiny." —*Maxwell Maltz*

633. If you're saving, you're succeeding. — *Steve Burkholder*

634. "The person who doesn't know where his next dollar is coming from usually doesn't know where his last dollar went."

635. "Annual income twenty pounds, annual expenditure nineteen six, result happiness."

636. "Doubt kills more dreams than failure ever will." — *Suzy Kassem*

637. Let him who would enjoy a good future waste none of his present. — *Roger Babson*

638. "We fall; we break; we fail. But then we rise; we heal; we overcome."

639. "Hardship often prepares an ordinary person for an extraordinary life." — *Christopher Markus*

640. "Your comfort zone will destroy you."

641. "Growth demands a temporary surrender of security. It may mean giving up familiar but limiting patterns, safe but unrewarding work, values no longer believed in, and relationships that have lost their meaning." *—John C. Maxwell*

642. "Be proud. You survived the days you thought you couldn't"

643. "Train your mind to be stronger than your feelings."

644. "Be brutally honest about the short term and optimistic and confident about the long term." *— Reed Hastings*

645. "If you are not actively seeking and creating opportunities, which always contain an element of risk, you are actually exposing yourself to more serious risks in the long term." *— Tony Buzan*

646. "Move with strategy, not emotion." *— Praveen M. Joshi*

647. "Take the risk or lose the chance."

648. "Just because it's not what you were expecting, doesn't mean it's not everything you need right now." — *Paulo Coelho*

649. "Giving back to the communities and institutions that helped us achieve success is a value we share and a privilege we embrace." — *Dinesh Paliwal*

650. "Your portfolio, leveraged or not, must be constructed in such a way that not only will it survive the bad days but thrive in a market meltdown."

651. "There is only one boss. The customer. And he can fire everybody in the company from the chairman on down, simply by spending his money somewhere else."

652. "When I had money everyone called me brother."

653. To achieve what 1% of the world's population has (financial freedom), you must be willing to do what only 1% dare to do...hard work and perseverance of the highest order. — *Manoj Arora*

654. "Don't worry about being famous or making money; the most important thing is being the best. You have to become a master of your craft, and everything else will come." — *Anastasia Soare*

655. "There is no optimal ratio for equity and debt distribution of a portfolio. Different times require different splits."

656. "Rich is a current income. Someone driving a $100,000 car is almost certainly rich because even if they purchased the car with debt you need a certain level of income to afford the monthly payment. Same with those who live in big homes. It's not hard to spot rich people. They often go out of their way to make themselves known."

657. "Don't let the fear of losing be greater than the excitement of winning."

658. "Passion is the genesis of genius." — *Tony Robbins*

659. "Stay committed to your decisions but stay flexible in your approach." — *Tony Robbins*

660. "The business schools reward difficult complex behavior more than simple behavior, but simple behavior is more effective

661. "Most of the assets can be a good investment if you buy at the right price."

662. "Being rich is having money; being wealthy is having time." — *Margaret Bonanno*

663. "The greatest gift you can give your children are the roots of responsibility and the wings of independence." — *Dennis Waitley*

664. "Don't save what is left after spending; spend what is left after saving."

665. "Every time you borrow money, you're robbing your future self."

666. "Believe that you are worthy of financial freedom. Do something you love and then all you ever have to do is be yourself to succeed." — *Jen Sincero*

667. "Saving is the foremost financial education we need, not finance."

668. "Wealth is hidden. It's income not spent. Wealth is the nice cars not purchased. The diamonds not bought. The watches not worn, the clothes forgone and the first—class upgrade declined. Wealth is financial assets that haven't yet been converted into the stuff you see. That's not how we think about wealth, because you can't contextualize what you can't see."

669. "It's better to have a partial interest in the Hope diamond than to own all of a rhinestone."

670. "When buying shares, ask yourself, would you buy the whole company?" — *Rene Rivkin*

671. "You make most of your money in a bear market, you just don't realize it at the time."

672. "Those who have knowledge of money make money their slave; but those who do not have knowledge of money becomes slave to it"

673. "A market downturn doesn't bother us. It is an opportunity to increase our ownership of great companies with great management at good prices."

674. "When trillions of dollars are managed by Wall Streeters charging high fees, it will usually be the managers who reap outsized profits, not the clients

675. "Success is the sum of small efforts, repeated day in and day out." — *Robert Collier*

676. "In the world of business, the people who are most successful are those who are doing what they love

677. "A sign of wealth: No longer needing an alarm clock to wake up."

678. "Given a 10% chance of a 100 times payoff, you should take that bet every time. — *Jeff Bezos*

679. "Focus on solving real problems and not on making money. There will be enough takers for your solutions. You will help make lives of some people better, and money will follow." — *Bhavish Aggarwal*

680. 86. "The time you spend monitoring your finances will pay off. You can make real money by cutting expenses and earning more interest on savings and investments. I'd challenge you to find a part—time job where you could potentially earn as much money for just an hour or two of your time.

— *Laura D. Adams*

681. "When you understand that your self—worth is not determined by your net—worth, then you'll have financial freedom."

—*Suze Orman*

682. "Management is doing things right; leadership is doing the right things".

683. "People respond well to those that are sure of what they want." — *Anna Wintour*

684. "To accumulate any wealth, you must invest at a growth rate higher than inflation."

685. "The best way to measure your investing success is not by whether you're beating the market but by whether you've put in place a financial plan and a behavioral discipline that are likely to get you where you want to go."

686. "If a business does well, the stock eventually follows."

687. "Without financial literacy, divorce rates soar, families rupture, and women stay with abusive men for financial security. A lack of jobs contributes to riots and illegal activity. Name any situation and it goes back to money. We need to focus on poverty eradication." — *John Hope Bryant*

688. "99% of all problems can be solved by money — and for the other 1% there's alcohol."

689. "Stop buying things you don't need, to impress people you don't even like."

690. "Remember that the only purpose of money is to get you what you want, so think hard about what you value and put it above money."

691. "It is a kind of spiritual snobbery that makes people think they can be happy without money."

692. "Wealth is the ability to fully experience life."

693. "I don't pay good wages because I have a lot of money; I have a lot of money because I pay good wages."

694. "The stock market is designed to transfer money from the active to the patient."

695. "Whether we're talking about socks or stocks, I like buying quality merchandise when it is marked down.

696. "If you live for having it all, what you have is never enough." — *Vicki Robin*

697. "Coming together is a beginning. Keeping together is progress. Working together is success."

698. "The investor of today does not profit from yesterday's growth

699. "Don't be fooled by the calendar. There are only as many days in the year as you make use of. One man gets only a week's value out of a year while another man gets a full year's value out of a week."

700. "Success in investing doesn't correlate with IQ. . . what you need is the temperament to control the urges that get other people into trouble in investing

701. "The most common cause of low prices is pessimism—sometimes pervasive, sometimes specific to a company or industry. We want to do business in such an environment, not because we like pessimism but because we like the prices it produces. It's optimism that is the enemy of the rational buyer

702. "Plans are only good intentions unless they immediately degenerate into hard work."

703. "It's amazing how fast later comes when you buy now."

704. "Good teams incorporate teamwork into their culture, creating the building blocks for success."

705. "Wealth is largely the result of habit."

706. "A modest rate—of—return can accumulate a fortune over time. You don't need to beat the market, do over—leveraging, or pick the best stock to be rich. You just need to earn a decent rate—of—return and let your money compound overtime."

707. "Someone's sitting in the shade today because someone planted a tree a long time ago."

708. "Don't tell me where your priorities are. Show me where you spend your money and I'll tell you what they are."

709. "Never invest in a business you cannot understand

710. "Money moves from those who do not manage it to those who do."

711. "Professional money managers are worried about their annual results and may take irrational decisions to protect their performance record. Individual investors have

712. "A budget isn't about restricting what you can spend. It gives you permission to spend without guilt or regret."

713. "Investors should remember that excitement and expenses are their enemies."

714. "Risk comes from not knowing what you are doing."

715. "You don't need to be a rocket scientist," goes a similar Buffett quote. "Investing is not a game where the guy with the 160 IQ beats the guy with 130 IQ."

716. "A budget is telling your money where to go instead of wondering where it went."

717. "…she wondered how she could have spent all that money and have nothing but clothes and accessories and a long list of men she never wanted to see again to show for it"

718. "If you make meaning, you'll make money." — *Suze Orman, financial*

advisor "Stop buying things you don't need, to impress people you don't even like." — *Suze Orman*

719. "Investing should be more like watching paint dry or watching grass grow. If you want excitement, take $800 and go to Las Vegas." — *Paul Samuelson*

720. "Time is the friend of the wonderful company, the enemy of the mediocre."

721. "Money, like emotions, is something you must control to keep your life on the right track." — *Natasha Munson*

722. "The speed of your success is limited only by your dedication and what you're willing to sacrifice"

723. "Financial literacy is just as important in life as the other basics." — *John W. Rogers, Jr., CEO Ariel Capital Management*

724. "The budget is not just a collection of numbers, but an expression of our values and aspirations." — *Jack Lew*

725. "If you have trouble imagining a 20% loss in the stock market, you shouldn't be in stocks."

726. "What counts for most people in investing vs saving is not how much they know, but rather how realistically they define what they don't know

727. "Planning is bringing the future into the present so that you can do something about it now." — *Alan Lakein*

728. "When you're working and making money, that's all good, but there has to be something that provides a substance, I think." — *Mekhi Phifer*

729. "Owning the stock market over the long term is a winner's game, but attempting to beat the market is a loser's game."

730. "…not doing what we love in the name of greed is very poor management of our lives

731. "Invest for the long haul. Don't get too greedy and don't get too scared."

732. "Money is good for nothing unless you know the value of it by experience."

733. "It is our choices that show what we truly are, far more than our abilities."

734. "You can only become truly accomplished at something you love. Don't make money your goal. Instead, pursue the things you love doing, and then do them so well that people can't take their eyes off you."

735. "Know what you own and know why you own it. — *Peter Lynch*

736. "Business is about making money but it is also about having fun, so get your character across." — *Peter Jones*

737. "In the business world, the rearview mirror is always clearer than the windshield

738. "No other ethnic group has even come close to matching the abilities and accomplishments of Jews."

739. "A great marriage is not when the 'perfect couple' comes together. It is when an imperfect couple learns to enjoy their differences." — *Dave Meurer*

740. "The individual investor should act consistently as an investor and not as a speculator."

741. "Money grows on the tree of persistence."

742. "As we spend money, we must have the courage to do a self—audit and admit what emotion is driving our spending." — *Deborah Smith Pegues*

743. "To be a successful investor, you don't need to take excessive risks and be involved in all sorts of financial instruments. You need to understand your risk appetite and understand a few asset classes well. Stay within your boundaries, and your wealth will grow at a decent pace."

744. "History provides a crucial insight regarding market crises: they are inevitable, painful and ultimately surmountable."

745. "Capital as such is not evil; it is its wrong use that is evil. Capital in some form or other will always be needed."

746. "I enjoy building something good and having a successful product and making money." — *Wayne Huizenga*

747. "Keep things simple and don't swing for the fences. When promised quick profits, respond with a quick no."

748. "No one can teach you how to be productive, whether it's in the office or at home, you have to do that for yourself and see what best works for you. There will be days when you will get to work on dozens of things in a day and there will be days when you will get none done."

749. "Should you find yourself in a chronically leaking boat, energy devoted to changing vessels is likely to be more productive than energy devoted to patching leaks

750. "The biggest risk of all is not taking one. — *Mellody Hobson*

751. "Far more money has been lost by investors trying to anticipate corrections than lost in the corrections themselves."

752. "Setting goals is the first step in turning the invisible into the visible." — *Tony Robbins*

753. "It's good to have money and the things that money can buy, but it's good, too, to check up once in a while and make sure that you haven't lost the things that money can't buy." — *George Lorimer*

754. "The more your money works for you, the less you have to work for money." — *Idowu Koyenikan*

755. "First rule of leadership: everything is your fault."

756. "Become so financially secure that you forget when payday is!"

757. "The best time to plant a tree is 20 years ago, the second—best time is now."

758. "Goals are dreams with deadlines."

759. "People do not decide their futures. They decide their habits, and their habits decide their futures."

760. "I like the art of making money more than making money." — *Richard Rawlings*

761. "Chains of habit are too light to be felt until they are too heavy to be broken

762. "I make no attempt to forecast the market—my efforts are devoted to finding undervalued securities."

763. "The correct period to judge performance is from a market peak to another peak or at least to the next all—time high."

764. "Like Warren, I had a considerable passion to get rich, not because I wanted Ferraris — I wanted the independence. I desperately wanted it."

765. "Expect the best. Prepare for the worst. Capitalize on what comes."

766. "Be careful to leave your sons well instructed rather than rich, for the hopes of the instructed are better than the wealth of the ignorant."

767. "There is an excellent characteristic of stock investment that it can only go to zero." — *Naved Abdali*

768. "Trade money for time, not time for money. You're going to run out of time first." — *Naval Ravikant*

769. "Far more money has been lost by investors trying to anticipate corrections, than lost in the corrections themselves." — *Peter Lynch*

770. "Opportunities come infrequently. When it rains gold, put out the bucket, not the thimble."

771. Peter Lynch reminds us, "You get recessions, you have stock market declines. If you don't understand that's going to happen, then you're not ready, you won't do well in the markets. " It is imperative to remember that economies are cyclical. Markets will recover in time, and it is important to make sure that you are going to be a part of those recoveries. It is vital to make sure you stay the course whenever declines or recessions hit

772. "Many folks think they aren't good at earning money, when what they don't know is how to use it."

773. "Remember that the stock market is a manic depressive.

774. "Money is always eager and ready to work for anyone who is ready to employ it." — *Idowu Koyenikan*

775. "Save money, and money will save you!"

776. "Timing, perseverance, and 10 years of trying will eventually make you look like an overnight success." — *Biz Stone (co—founder of Twitter)*

777. "What we really want to do is what we are really meant to do. When we do what we are meant to do, money comes to us, doors open for us, we feel useful, and the work we do feels like play to us. " —*Julia Cameron*

778. "American business — and consequently a basket of stocks — is virtually certain to be worth far more in the years ahead

779. "The poor and the middle—class work for money. The rich have money work for them."

780. "The more your money works for you, the less you have to work for money."

781. "If you would be wealthy, think of saving as well as getting."

782. "If investors do not know or never attempt to know the fair value, they can pay any price. More often, the price they pay is far greater than the actual value."

783. "There seems to be some perverse human characteristic that likes to make easy things difficult

784. "Do not follow where the path may lead. Go instead where there is no path and leave a trail." — *Muriel Strode*

785. Another piece of great advice comes from Carmen Reinhart, who says: "If there is

one common theme to the vast range of the world's financial crises, it is that excessive debt accumulation, whether by the government, banks, corporations, or consumers, often poses greater systemic risks than it seems during a boom. " During periods of prosperity we can be more likely to get into debts, which simply are not sustainable in the future, so do be aware of this

786. "When money will lose its value, it will be easy to lend."

787. "The most important thing is to invest. The second most important thing is to buy well."

788. "Balancing your money is the key to having enough."

789. "Capital withdrawals by investors can torpedo investment strategies of money managers at the worst possible time."

790. "Leadership is the art of getting someone else to do something you want done because he wants to do it."

791. "Time is more valuable than money. You can get more money, but you cannot get more time."

792. "Whoever said money can't buy happiness, didn't know where to go shopping."

793. "The best financial advice I can give to someone who's overwhelmed with their finances is "ask for help!""

794. "Making money from money is like aerobatics." *— Alisher Usmanov*

795. "If you don't value your time, neither will others. Stop giving away your time and talents. Value what you know and start charging for it." *—Kim Garst*

796. "It's not your salary that makes you rich; it's your spending habits." *— Charles A. Jaffe*

797. "Don't make money, create wealth. Making money is easy. Being able to create and sustain wealth is what will set you apart from the rest."

798. "Most people get interested in stocks when everyone else is. The time to get interested is when no one else is. You can't buy what is popular and do well

799. "Spending money is much more difficult than making money." — *Jack Ma*

800. "Money does not buy you happiness, but lack of money certainly buys you misery."

801. "The Talmud says that "blessed is He who has created all these to serve me." German politician Julius Streicher said, "It is an open secret that Jews do not work, but rather let others work for them."

802. "A budget doesn't limit your freedom; it gives you freedom."

803. "Making money is a common sense. It's not rocket science. But unfortunately, when it comes to money, common sense is uncommon."

804. Whenever we spend money instead of investing it, we are actually taking from ourselves—we are taking both the time we spend to make the money and the future freedom it can buy. *—Grant Sabatier*

805. "No amount of money or success can take the place of time spent with your family."

806. "The most important decision about your goals is not what you're willing to do to achieve them, but what you are willing to give up."

807. "Returns matter a lot. It's our capital. — *Abigail Johnson*

808. "Good management is the art of making problems so interesting and their solutions so constructive that everyone wants to get to work and deal with them." — *Paul Hawken*

809. "Invest with the end in mind." *—Joe Saul—Sehy*

810. "Traders, as a group, always fall short of investors."

811. "A great company is not a great investment if you pay too much for the stock." *— Benjamin Graham*

812. "Annual performance means nothing to individual investors."

813. "Management is about arranging and telling. Leadership is about nurturing and enhancing."

814. "That man is richest whose pleasures are cheapest."

815. "There are so many people out there who will tell you that you can't. What you have to do is turn around and tell them watch me."

816. "None of us is as smart as all of us." — *Ken Blanchard*

817. "Wealth is like sea—water; the more we drink, the thirstier we become; and the same is true of fame."

818. "Travel continues to broaden the mind and slim the wallet."

819. "The most important investment you can make is in yourself."

820. "A fool and his money are soon parted." — *Thomas Tusser*

821. "Predicting rain doesn't count, building the ark does."

822. "An ounce of gold will always be an ounce of gold regardless of the length of possession. The short—term value will go up or down, but gold prices will follow the general inflation rate in the long run."

823. "The stock market is filled with individuals who know the price of everything, but the value of nothing. — *Phillip Fisher*

824. "In medieval Europe, aristocrats spent their money carelessly on extravagant luxuries, whereas peasants lived frugally, minding every penny. Today, the tables have turned. The rich take great care managing their assets and investments, while the less well—heeled go into debt buying cars and televisions they don't really need." — *Yuval Noah Harari*

825. "The three most important words in investing are margin of safety

826. "Why not invest your assets in the companies you really like? As Mae West said, 'Too much of a good thing can be wonderful. "

827. "A leader must have the courage to act against an expert's advice."

828. "Do something today that your future self will thank you for."

829. "Try to save something while your salary is small; it's impossible to save after you begin to earn more."

830. "Never stand begging for that which you have the power to earn."

831. "Plans are worthless. Planning is essential."

832. "You get recessions, you have stock market declines. If you don't understand what's going to happen, then you're not ready, you won't do well in the markets. — *Peter Lynch*

833. "You can't have financial freedom when you can't tame your desire to have more stuff in your life. You are a hoarder in the making."

834. "We simply attempt to be fearful when others are greedy and to be greedy only when others are fearful

835. "How many millionaires do you know who have become wealthy by investing in savings accounts? I rest my case." — *Robert G. Allen*

836. "Although some popular religious texts such as the New Testament, Quran, Bhagavad Gita, Tao Te Ching, or Tibetan Book of the Dead contain interesting insights and stories, it is the Jewish religious texts such as the Old Testament (Hebrew Scriptures) that contain valuable information on acquiring wealth."

837. "Budgeting only has one rule; Do not go over budget."

838. "Wall Street is the only place that people ride to in a Rolls Royce to get advice from those who take the subway

839. "Today people who hold cash equivalents feel comfortable. They shouldn't. They have opted for a terrible long—term asset, one that pays virtually nothing and is certain to depreciate in value."

840. "Vision without action is a dream. Action without vision is simply passing the time. Action with Vision is making a positive difference."

841. 496. "I'm not a perfect parent, but I'm exactly the parent my child needs."

842. "Money is multiplied in practical value depending on the number of W's you control in your life: what you do, when you do it, where you do it, and with whom you do it."

843. "Financial fitness is not a pipe dream or a state of mind. It's a reality if you are willing to pursue it and embrace it." —***Will Robinson, author***

844. "Wide diversification is only required when investors do not understand what they are doing

845. "What is important is family, friends, giving back to your community and finding meaning in life." — *Adrian Grenier*

846. "Management's job is to convey leadership's message in a compelling and inspiring way. Not just in meetings, but also by example."

847. "No matter how great the talent or efforts, some things just take time. You can't produce a baby in one month by getting nine women pregnant."

848. "It's simple arithmetic: "Your income can grow only to the extent you do".

849. "Before you speak, listen. Before you write, think. Before you spend, earn. Before you invest, investigate. Before you criticize, wait. Before you pray, forgive. Before you quit, try. Before you retire, save. Before you die, give."

850. "Stay the course…. Changing your strategy at the wrong time can be the single most devastating mistake you can make as an investor."

851. "It's good to have money and the things that money can buy, but it's good, too, to check up once in a while and make sure that you haven't lost the things that money can't buy." — *George Lorimer*

852. "Real wealth is not about money. Real wealth is: not having to go to meetings, not having to spend time with jerks, not being locked into status games, not feeling like you have to say "yes", not worrying about others claiming your time and energy. Real wealth is about freedom."

853. "Tell me who your heroes are and I'll tell you who you'll turn out to be."

854. "Wealth is not his that has it, but his that enjoys it."

855. "Do not take yearly results too seriously. Instead, focus on four or five—year averages."

856. "With a good perspective on history, we can have a better understanding of the past and present, and thus a clear vision of the future. — *Carlos Slim Helu*

857. "A wise person should have money in their head, but not in their heart."

858. "Focus on results only. Agree with every department/team/person on what is their KPI (key performance indicator). The focus has to be clear, and there has to be a numerical goal agreed upon too. After you have done this, you don't really care if somebody is working 8 hours a day (which btw is bullshit anyway, you can rarely do over 6 hours of productive work in a day. I know, I Toggled it), you just follow up how people are progressing with their KPIs. The approach is very black & white. It doesn't allow anyone to hide between busy—work, only results matter."

859. "Budgeting isn't about limiting yourself — it's about making the things that excite you possible."

860. "Thousands of experts study overbought indicators, head—and—shoulder patterns, put—call ratios, the Fed's policy on money supply…and they can't predict markets with any useful consistency, any more than the gizzard squeezers could tell the Roman emperors when the Huns would attack."

861. "Most of what we call management consists of making it difficult for people to get their work done."

862. "The stock market is a device to transfer money from the impatient to the patient."

863. "How many millionaires do you know who have become wealthy by investing in savings accounts? I rest my case." — ***Robert G. Allen***

864. "Knowledge is power: you hear it all the time but knowledge is not power. It's only potential power. It only becomes power when we apply it and use it. Somebody who reads a book and doesn't apply it, they're at no advantage over someone who's illiterate. None of it works unless you work. We have to do our part. If knowing is half the battle,

action is the second half of the battle."
— *Jim Kwik*

865. "A man who pays his bills on time is soon forgotten."

866. "A budget tells us what we can't afford, but it doesn't keep us from buying it."

867. "Bottoms in the investment world don't end with four—year lows; they end with 10— or 15—year lows. — *Jim Rogers*

868. "The problem for many of us is that it is easy to find rich role models. It's harder to find wealthy ones because by definition their success is more hidden.

869. "If you are inexperienced, start with a fraction of your money. Don't play with money that is not yours."

870. "Never depend on a single income. Make an investment to create a second source.

871. "How many millionaires do you know who have become wealthy by investing in savings accounts? I rest my case."

872. "Happiness is not in the mere possession of money; it lies in the joy of achievement, in the thrill of creative effort."

873. "Compound interest is the eighth wonder of the world. He who understands it, earns it; he who doesn't, pays it."

874. "The enemy of every investor is fear, greed, and impatience."

875. "The person who doesn't know where his next dollar is coming from usually doesn't know where his last dollar went."

876. "It doesn't matter about money; having it, not having it. Or having clothes, or not having them. You're still left alone with yourself in the end."

877. "Though tempting, trying to time the market is a loser's game. $10,000 continuously invested in the market over the past 20 years grew to more than $48,000. If you missed just the best 30 days, your investment was reduced to $9,900.1"

878. "Never invest in a business you cannot understand. "

879. "On the margin of safety, which means, don't try and drive a 9,800—pound truck over a bridge that says it's, you know, capacity: 10,000 pounds. But go down the road a little bit and find one that says, capacity: 15,000 pounds."

880. "The most contrarian thing of all is not to oppose the crowd but to think for yourself." — *Peter Thiel*

881. "Investing should be more like watching paint dry or watching grass grow. If you want excitement, take $800 and go to Las Vegas."

882. "Formal education will make you a living; self—education will make you a fortune."

883. "How many millionaires do you know who have become wealthy by investing in savings accounts? I rest my case." — *Robert G. Allen*

884. "Beware the investment activity that produces applause; the great moves are usually greeted by yawns."

885. "Money is like love; it kills slowly and painfully the one who withholds it, and enlivens the other who turns it on his fellow man."

886. "Succeeding in business is not just about making money." — *Daniel Snyder*

887. "We cannot live without money, but we can live without a bank account."

888. "Be bold enough to use your voice, brave enough to listen to your heart, and strong enough to live the life you have always imagined."

889. "Budgeting is not just for people who do not have enough money. It is for everyone who wants to ensure that their money is enough."

890. "Spend your money on the things money can buy. Spend your time on the things money can't buy."

891. "If you are in the world of business, that means you are in the business of making money." — *Stephen A. Smith*

892. "If you haven't found it yet, keep looking. Don't settle. As with all matters of the heart, you'll know when you find it." — *Steve Jobs*

893. "What we learn from history is that people don't learn from history

894. "A budget is more than just a series of numbers on a page; it is an embodiment of our values."

895. "If you want to know what a man is really like, take notice of how he acts when he loses money."

896. "When you work on something that only has the capacity to make you 5 dollars, it does not matter how much harder you work — the most you will make is 5 dollars."

897. "When you deposit your money with a bank, you are giving your money to the bank on loan, and your money is only as secure as your bank is."

898. "Unless commitment is made, there are only promises and hopes; but no plans." — *Peter F. Drucker*

899. "Invest for the long haul. Don't get too greedy and don't get too scared." — *Shelby M. C. Davis*

900. "Jews believe that people are creators, not consumers. The role of humans is to improve and perfect God's creations through work, creation, and innovation."

901. "The key to investing is not assessing how much an industry is going to affect society, or how much it will grow, but rather determining the competitive advantage of any given company and, above all, the durability of that advantage."

902. "The idea that a bell rings to signal when to get into or out of the stock market is simply not credible. After nearly fifty years in this business, I don't know anybody who has done it successfully and consistently. I don't even know anybody who knows anybody who has."

903. "Price is what you pay. Value is what you get"

904. "Traders try to beat the market but don't understand that cumulatively they are the market."

905. "Many people take no care of their money till they come nearly to the end of it, and others do just the same with their time."

906. "He who loses money, loses much; He who loses a friend, loses much more; He who loses faith, loses all."

907. "It's not the employer who pays the wages. Employers only handle the money. It's the customer who pays the wages."

908. "Expect the best, plan for the worst, and prepare to be surprised."

909. "The function of economic forecasting is to make astrology look respectable."

910. "The key to making money is to stay invested." — *Suze Orman*

911. "Investing should be more like watching paint dry or watching grass grow. If you want excitement, take $800 and go to Las Vegas. — *Paul Samuelson*

912. "It's pretty much how we get anything added to the curriculum. When parents said children needed to be computer literate, the schools started responding. The same thing is true of basic financial literacy." — *Elizabeth Warren, United States Senator*

913. Financial stability is much more about doing the best with what you have and not about achieving a certain level of income. — *Erik Wecks*

914. "It's not whether you're right or wrong that's important, but how much money you make when you're right and how much you lose when you're wrong." — *George Soros*

915. "It's not whether you're right or wrong that's important, but how much money you make when you're right and how much you lose when you're wrong." —*George Soros*

916. "There is a difference between broke and being poor. Being broke is a temporary economic condition, but being poor is a disabling frame of mind and a depressed condition of your spirit, and you must vow to never, ever be poor again." —*John Hope Bryant,* **Operation Hope CEO**

917. "Both poverty and riches are the offspring of thought." — *Napolean Hill*

918. "A team is successful only when they have a common goal. Not only does this goal need to be set, but it also has to be communicated to each team member."

919. "To get rich, you have to be making money while you're asleep." -- *David Bailey*

920. "You Can't Have a Million Dollar Dream With a Minimum Wage Work Ethic." — *Stephen C. Hogan*

921. "The government wants to keep the capital markets healthy and thriving. They will do whatever in their power to avoid or reverse a recession."

922. "Debt is like any other trap, easy enough to get into, but hard enough to get out of."
   —Josh Billings

923. "Making money is a hobby that will complement any other hobbies you have, beautifully." *— Scott Alexander*

924. "Wealth does not make people happy, but positive increases in wealth may."

925. "Making money is easy. It is. The difficult thing in life is not making it; it's keeping it." *—John McAfee*

926. "To acquire money requires valor, to keep money requires prudence, and to spend money well is an art."

927. "Aren't we killing ourselves — our health, our relationships, our sense of joy, and wonder for our jobs? We are sacrificing our lives for money, but it's happening so slowly that we barely notice."

928. "With a good perspective on history, we can have a better understanding of the past and present, and thus a clear vision of the future." — *Carlos Slim Helu*

929. "Waiting helps you as an investor and a lot of people just can't stand to wait. If you didn't get the deferred gratification gene, you've got to work very hard to overcome that."

930. "Our goals can only be reached through a vehicle of a plan, in which we must fervently believe, and upon which we must vigorously act. There is no other route to success."

931. "Money, like emotions, is something you must control to keep your life on the right track."

932. "An investor should act as though he had a lifetime decision card with just twenty punches on it

933. "Courage taught me no matter how bad a crisis gets. . . any sound investment will eventually pay off. *— Carlos Slim Helu*

934. "You must gain control over your money or the lack of it will forever control you."

935. "Debt is one person's liability, but another person's asset." *—Paul Krugman, economist*

936. "The most important thing to do if you find yourself in a hole is to stop digging."

937. "Here's how I think of my money — as soldiers — I send them out to war every day. I want them to take prisoners and come home, so there's more of them." *— Kevin O'Leary*

938. "Children are great imitators. So give them something great to imitate."

939. "The first step to financial freedom is to understand yourself. The next step is understanding your relationship with money."

940. "You are 30+, you can't keep blaming your lack of financial literacy on your high school teachers."

941. "A budget is your own roadmap to your financial success. Can't get mad if you never asked for directions."

942. "There are no get—rich—quick schemes. Building wealth takes time, effort, and discipline."

943. "Never trust advice from people who never show their hands"

944. "Debt is a thief that robs you of your time, your energy, and your freedom."

945. "Let them struggle. Not everyone wants your version of Success."

946. "Most influencers copy—paste snippets of financial literacy. Seek the big picture."

947. "The only way to get ahead financially isn't to live below your means. The goal is to change for the better."

948. "Financial freedom is not about having a lot of money. That's the tweet."

949. "Investing in three ways: in your Education, in your Network, and in the Market."

950. "Emergencies hit every 4 years or so. You might as well prep for the next one."

951. "Fortunately, I learned from multiple sources. Some are too devoted to their first source."

952. "Approach building wealth with the same enthusiasm you had when you were spending it away."

953. "You don't want to just be a consumer, you want to be a participant." — *Joe Rogan*

954. "You only regret the workouts you didn't do." — *Joe Rogan*

955. "Don't let the noise of others' opinions drown out your own inner voice. And most importantly, have the courage to follow your heart and intuition." — *Steve Jobs*

956. "I think frugality drives innovation, just like other constraints do. One of the only ways to get out of a tight box is to invent your way out." —*Jeff Bezos*

957. "Whether you've found your calling, or if you're still searching, passion should be the fire that drives your life's work." — *Michael Dell*

958. "The most dangerous poison is the feeling of achievement. The antidote is to every evening think what can be done better tomorrow." — *Ingvar Kamprad*

959. "Money is misunderstood. The fact is if you want to be successful the money will follow you. If you are a doctor, something else will follow you. If you are successful, there is an accompaniment and If your goal is just to make money, you won't succeed. Money is a commodity to use, not to be dictated by." — *Frank Lowy*

960. "Money is just a consequence. I always say to my team, 'Don't worry too much about profitability. If you do your job well, the profitability will come." — *Bernard Arnault*

961. "No action is too small when it comes to changing the world… I'm inspired every time I meet an entrepreneur who is succeeding against all odds" — *Cyril Ramaphosa*

962. "I think it's very important to have a feedback loop, where you're constantly thinking about what you've done and how you could be doing it better. I think that's the single best piece of advice: constantly think about how you could be doing things better and questioning yourself." — *Elon Musk*

963. "The biggest risk is not taking any risk. In a world that is changing really quickly, the only strategy that is guaranteed to fail is not taking risks." — *Mark Zuckerberg*

964. "Vision is perhaps our greatest strength… it has kept us alive to the power and continuity of thought through the centuries, it makes us peer into the future and lends shape to the unknown." — *Li Ka—Shing*

965. "I'll keep working until the end." — *Amancio Ortega*

966. "Most people give up just when they're about to achieve success. They quit on the one—yard line. They give up at the last minute of the game one foot from a winning touchdown." — *H. Ross Perot*

967. "If you are in business, you are not enjoying. You are working" — *Carlos Slim Helu*

968. "I believe people have to follow their dreams — I did." — *Larry Ellison*

969. "Relentlessly strive to come up with new and better products and produce them more efficiently than the alternatives." — *Charles Koch*

970. "When the rate of change outside is more than what is inside, be sure that the end is near." — *Azim Premji*

971. "Don't think you are unstoppable or foolproof. Don't think that the only way your business will work is through perfection. And don't aim for perfection. Aim for success." — *Eike Batista*

972. "Failure is not the outcome — failure is not trying. Don't be afraid to fail." — *Sara Blakely*

973. "Lots of companies don't succeed over time. What do they fundamentally do wrong? They usually miss the future."

— *Larry Page*

974. "For me, businesses are like buses. You stand on a corner and you don't like where the first bus is going? Wait ten minutes and take another. Don't like that one? They'll just keep coming. There's no end to buses or businesses." — *Sheldon Adelson*

975. "Patience is a key element of success." — *Bill Gates*

976. "Every time I make a mistake with a company, I write it out and try to figure out why it happened." — *Garrett Champ*

977. "You can worry about the competition or you can focus on what's ahead of you and drive fast." —*Jack Dorsey*

978. "Have fun. The game is a lot more enjoyable when you're trying to do more than just <u>make money</u>." — *Tony Hsieh*

979. "I learned from my dad that change and experimentation are constants and important. You have to keep trying new things." — *S. Robson Walton*

980. "Hard work certainly goes a long way. These days a lot of people work hard, so you have to make sure you work even harder and really dedicate yourself to what you are doing and setting out to achieve." — *Lakshmi Mittal*

981. "I feel like in a world where we all try to figure out our place and our purpose here, your passions are one of your most obvious guides." — *Nick Woodman*

982. "I think that our fundamental belief is that for us growth is a way of life and we have to grow at all times." — *Mukesh Ambani*

983. "In Life, you don't get anywhere or do anything you hope to without some sort of sacrifice." — *Stephen Saad*

984. "I am not a person who pursues luxury. I am not like those people who, once they have money, compulsively squander it or show it off." — *Wang Jianlin*

985. "I realized that in a lot of failures, there are a lot of opportunities." — *Clive Palmer*

986. "Do the things others don't want to do." — *John Paul DeJoria*

987. "There has to be a balance in life. A balance of business, family, and the opportunity to learn and teach." — *Chuck Feeney*

988. "There are very few people in the world who get to build a business like this. I think trading that for some short—term gain isn't very interesting." — *Evan Spiegel*

989. "Never give up. Today is hard, tomorrow will be worse, but the day after tomorrow will be sunshine." — *Jack Ma*

990. "If we go to work at 8 a.m. and go home at 5 p.m., this is not a high—tech company and Alibaba will never be successful. If we have that kind of 8—to—5 spirit, then we should just go and do something else." —*Jack Ma*

991. "If you are hardworking and determined, you will make it and that's the bottom line. I don't believe in an easy way through." — *Isabel dos Santos*

992. "The best way to become a billionaire is to help a billion people." — *Peter H. Diamandis*

993. "Be obsessed or be average." — *Grant Cardone*

994. "America is built around this premise that you can do it, and there are an awful lot of people who are unlikely to have done it." — *Michael Bloomberg*

995. "I think when it comes to decisions. I try not to be emotional. To drown out the noise and look at the important facts." — *David Tepper*

996. "The only way you are going to have success is to have lots of failures first." — *Sergey Brin*

997. "I think frugality drives innovation, just like other constraints do. One of the only ways to get out of a tight box is to invent your way out." — *Jeff Bezos*

998. "If you are born poor it's not your mistake, but if you die poor it's your mistake." — *Bill Gates*

999. "The biggest risk is not taking any risk. In a world that is changing really quickly, the only strategy that is guaranteed to fail is not taking risks." — *Mark Zuckerberg*

1000. "I'll keep working until the end." — *Amancio Ortega*

1001. "Relentlessly strive to come up with new and better products and produce them more efficiently than the alternatives." — *Charles Koch*

1002. "America is built around this premise that you can do it, and there are an awful lot of people who are unlikely to have done it who did." — *Michael Bloomberg*

1003. "I believe people have to follow their dreams — I did." — *Larry Ellison*

1004. "I learned from my dad that change and experimentation are constants and important. You have to keep trying new things." — *S. Robson Walton*

1005. "I have had all of the disadvantages required for success." — *Larry Ellison*

1006. Let him who would enjoy a good future waste none of his present. — *Roger Babson*

1007. Screw it, Let's do it! — *Richard Branson*

1008. "All you have in business is your reputation. So, it's very important that you keep your word." — *Richard Branson*

1009. "If wealth was the inevitable result of hard work and enterprise, every woman in Africa would be a millionaire." — *George Monbiot*

About Kharis Publishing:

Kharis Publishing, an imprint of Kharis Media LLC, is a leading Christian and inspirational book publisher based in Aurora, Chicago metropolitan area, Illinois. Kharis' dual mission is to give voice to under-represented writers (including women and first-time authors) and equip orphans in developing countries with literacy tools. That is why, for each book sold, the publisher channels some of the proceeds into providing books and computers for orphanages in developing countries so that these kids may learn to read, dream, and grow. For a limited time, Kharis Publishing is accepting unsolicited queries for nonfiction (Christian, self-help, memoirs, business, health and wellness) from qualified leaders, professionals, pastors, and ministers.

Learn more at: https://kharispublishing.com/